FROM THE LION'S MOUTH

A Journey Along the Indus

Iain Campbell

Bradt

First published in the UK in July 2019 by
Bradt Travel Guides Ltd
31a High Street, Chesham, Bucks HP5 1BW, England
www.bradtguides.com

Print edition published in the USA by The Globe Pequot Press Inc,
PO Box 480, Guilford, Connecticut 06437-0480

Text copyright © 2019 Iain Campbell
Map © Bradt Travel Guides 2019
Project managed by Anna Moores
Edited by Samantha Cook
Cover illustration by Neil Gower
Layout and typesetting by Ian Spick
Route map by David McCutcheon FBCart.S
Production managed by Sue Cooper, Bradt & Jellyfish Print Solutions

ISBN: 978 1 78477 160 7

British Library Cataloguing in Publication Data
A catalogue record for this book is available from the British Library
Digital conversion by www.dataworks.co.in
Printed in the UK

ACKNOWLEDGEMENTS

I would like to acknowledge the assistance of many friends who have read early drafts, encouraged me and cajoled me throughout the writing process. Heartfelt thanks to Anne Riach, Douglas Riach, Simon Crawshaw, Hector Cook, Tom Miller, Kieron Quirke, Krishnan Narayanan, Duncan Stewart, Charles Ogilvie and Peter Blair.

Without my agent Jennifer Barclay, this book might never have seen the light of day. Her encouragement and advice have been invaluable. Thanks too, to everyone at Bradt for their expertise and guidance.

I am indebted to all the friends I made along my journey in Pakistan and India. It would be impossible to name you all here but your kindness and hospitality, particularly when I was tired, ill or lost, was extraordinary. *Mera dost, Shukriya.*

Nobody has been more important to me in the pursuit of this project than the members of my family. I want to thank my parents for instilling in me, early on, a love for wild places and for their help and understanding over the years. Most importantly I want to thank my loving and supportive wife Sinead, and my three wonderful children, Lachlan, Niall Angus and Magnus, who provide unending inspiration.

DEDICATION

For Sinead, with love

ABOUT THE AUTHOR

Iain Campbell has been fascinated by mountains for as long as he can remember and has travelled widely in the mountains of his home country of Scotland and further afield. He studied history at Oxford University where he specialised in medieval religious history. In 2002 he decided to combine these interests by travelling to the holy mountains of Asia. His first book *With Unblest Feet* tells the story of a journey among the mountain pilgrims of the Silk Road. It was while travelling the Tibetan section of this route that he was inspired to follow the course of the Indus, one of the great rivers of the Indian subcontinent, which runs from its source in Tibet to its mouth near Karachi in Pakistan. *From the Lion's Mouth*, his second book, is the story of this journey. Iain lives with his family in Edinburgh and continues to travel frequently to Asia.

NOTE ON TRANSLITERATION

Urdu is generally written using the Nastaliq script, a modified form of the Arabic alphabet. In this book I have transliterated any Urdu words phonetically using the Roman alphabet and have generally followed the system used in the *Essential Urdu Dictionary* (John Murray, 2015). For the sake of simplicity in the text I have excluded phonetic notations. For local dialects and place names of minor settlements where I could find no reference on English-language maps I have simply written phonetically how they sounded to me at the time.

CONTENTS

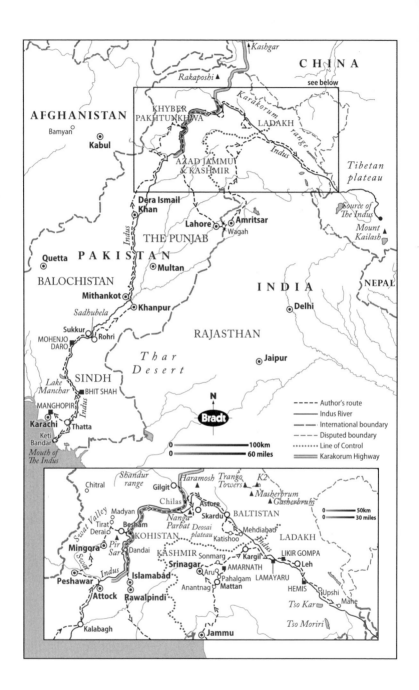

PROLOGUE

A year before this journey began I stood on a dusty pass above a Tibetan valley and looked down into a gathering gloom. Behind me was the darkening bulk of Mount Kailash, a holy mountain for Buddhists and Hindus. All day I had walked round that unclimbed, sacred mountain, among yak trains and Buddhist pilgrims. High above me the ferocious wind on the 22,000ft summit created a constant arc of spindrift against the blue of the sky. But in the dying light of evening I walked away from the path to look for something else. I walked away from where the vertical scratches of the north face met the valley and we had made our camp, past the buttery hive of a monastery that was cocooned in the fold of a cliff. Past the black felt tents where the yak herders' dogs barked and pulled their chains taut at my approaching footsteps. The track faded where it was cut with tongues of scree.

I caught up with some yak herders. They did not speak English but I knew the Tibetan for what I was looking for.

'*Senge Khabab, Senge Khabab?*' I said, 'River from the Lion's Mouth', the Tibetan name for the source of the Indus River, one of the five great rivers of the Indian subcontinent. They repeated the words back to me, and more words in Tibetan that I couldn't understand, pointing far away beyond rolling foothills to a distant crease in the land, where perhaps a river turned west, gathered streams and left Tibet. I think they were telling me I wouldn't get to Senge Khabab that evening, it was too far. They held up their fingers and pointed to their animals. I would need two days, and food and yaks.

In my naivety I had thought that I would come across the source close to the path that encircled the mountain, because I had read that Mount Kailash is the source of four great rivers: the Brahmaputra, the Ganges, the Sutlej and the Indus. But the ridges and ice-encrusted spurs of Kailash were on a Himalayan scale, stretching dozens of miles from the summit.

It was near sunset and cold air was running down the mountains. I stopped walking and sat on a rock. I would not see Senge Khabab on that trip. But this view had set something alight inside me.

An idea was conceived as I sat on that rock and I glowed with the excitement of it. I would travel the Indus, mouth to source. I watched the yak herders turn to shadows, then specks, then invisible far away on the scree, but I could still hear the clack of hooves on rock. I began planning a trip that would take me all along this river.

I originally hoped to do it by boat. I researched the possibility of shipping a flat-pack Canadian canoe out to Pakistan which I planned to assemble in the north and sail all the way down to Karachi. But a brief preparatory trip to Pakistan a few months later showed how unwise this would be. In the north the river comprised miles and miles of impossible rapids and in the south the river was so wide and prone to flooding that there were few towns visible from the water, which would make navigation impossible and the journey perhaps rather monotonous. Instead I decided to follow it more loosely by train and bus and on foot and use its route to make my way up Pakistan into India and Tibet.

PART I PAKISTAN

THE PLAINS:
SINDH AND THE PUNJAB

CHAPTER 1

KETI BANDAR

I had decided to follow the Indus from mouth to source, but it took me some time to work out exactly where I should begin. In the end I settled for a town called Keti Bandar, which on my not very accurate map looked to be the furthest south of the small towns built on the Indus delta.

After two days of buses and hitched rides from Karachi I stood in what passed for the bazaar in Keti Bandar: a couple of provision stores and a fly-infested teahouse. The town was surrounded by flood banks against the tides; inside the walls I could see stinking pools of green water fringed with litter and scum.

A man approached me.

'*Aap kya kar rahe hai?*' What are you doing here?

'*Main saiyah hai.*' I am a tourist.

'A tourist? We don't have tourists here. There is nothing to see.'

This was the only time I heard this in Pakistan. Even in the most obscure places, very early on in the conversation after I had told them my nationality, the details of my family, my salary and whether I was married, people would tell me about the other foreigners who had visited, their clothes and what machines they had brought with them. But no-one came to Keti Bandar.

'Foreigners go to Karachi. I have seen them there. I am a fisherman. My name is Gani.'

'Peace be unto you. I want to go out in a boat. Do you have one?'

Gani took me to the middleman who bought his daily catch. I didn't see why he wanted me to negotiate the price of a couple of hours in his boat through the middleman (who would inevitably take a cut just as he did with the catch) but maybe it was just force of habit, or he didn't trust himself to make a deal.

The price agreed, we rolled up our trousers and slithered across the tidal mudflats towards the narrow wooden fishing boats, which leaned on their sides with their outboard motors upraised like beaks. The mud sprouted between my toes on tiny stalks and stuck in loamy clumps to my heels. The clay of the riverbed is fine here because only the lightest particles of silt are carried all the way down to the delta. In the mountains the river has the strength to roll boulders along its bed so that it rumbles like thunder, but down in the flatlands of Sindh, it barely has the strength to move itself and it can only support the dust that makes this grey delta slurry.

We chugged out slowly into the muddy stream and for ten minutes Gani did not speak. I imagined the channels were complicated and he needed to pay attention. Then he smiled.

'All Pakistan's shit is here.'

He drew his arm across the bank of silt. 'We are living on Pakistan's shit.'

Up until then he had sat looking along the bow of the boat, eyes half closed against the salt in the air, but now his arm moved expansively and slowly and the words were orated with his lips drawn back from his teeth. He seemed to be imitating the grandiose delivery of a village official or one of the TV imams. 'We are living on shit.' It sounded like something that had been said before. Some insightful and cynical line from Keti Bandar's teahouse wit. But in a way it was true. Only two cities in Pakistan process their sewage. The rest is released untreated into the Indus River whose watershed covers 95 per cent of Pakistan's population. I nodded.

He started laughing and when he turned away from me to face the bow again he was still laughing, with open mouth tilted up-the-way so the gory soup of chewed betel nut, that ubiquitous subcontinental stimulant, did not dribble out. His laugh was lost in the skin-slapping sound of the motor. His shoulders subsided forward and the lids of his eyes brushed down. He assumed the drowsy pose that I imagine he would be in for most of his working day, eyes shielded against sun and salt, hand behind him on the motor. When he spat into the sea the brown water went red with betel nut juice, then brown again.

I was tired too after travelling for hours through Sindh on the roof of a bus. It had been a day of flatness and heat. A 360-degree horizon, level and unblemished; the sky felt low. The only punctuation marks on the dust were the houses and a few trees, but neither stretched high enough to interrupt the misted line where the sky finished. The houses were insubstantial wooden frames clad in rectangles of reed matting. Channels ran off from canals through the fields and the leaves of the trees were ingrained with the same dust they grew in because around here the water seldom comes from the sky. Their powdered leaves made them seem ghostly and not quite alive.

Water buffalo, black shiny sacks of bones and belly, stood motionless and enduring in the shade of spindly trees or wallowed, only eyes and nose visible, in the pools of standing water. Camels wandered past, weighed under bundles of sugarcane. Their pouts and upheld chins gave them an appearance of supreme arrogance, as if this work was beneath them and they were merely humouring the farmers that led them – *these chaotic bundles of foliage – these were not our idea…*

The bus eventually terminated and to continue towards the coast and Keti Bandar I had to take a pick-up truck stacked with oil drums, sacks of food and several other passengers. The trees were replaced by low coarse scrub, then the ground went bare. This was the salt marsh.

The road was built on an embankment above the marsh. The divisions between land and water were blurred. I kept thinking I could see the river across the white marsh but when we got closer it would turn out to be a slick of standing water or the glassiness of hot air. The earth and the water were evenly mixed and rolled out perfectly flat. The road just pointed itself in the general direction of Keti Bandar and went straight.

Periodically the passengers banged on the roof of the driver's cab to make it stop, '*Ji, bas bas bas*', they shouted. 'Enough'. They walked away along tiny paths only visible due to their dry dusting of salt, meandering across the marsh to houses that I could not see and couldn't imagine a reason for. Nothing grew and there were no animals there.

There was something apocalyptic about the very end of Pakistan. The river was finishing, the land was too wet to hold a road. Everything was dissolving and collapsing back on itself in the flat white heat. It felt prehistoric. Here there were no continents; earth and water had not yet become separated from the primeval soup, and the world was not yet ready for life.

Gani's house was on one of the silt bars looking towards Keti Bandar. On the way over there I asked him to point out which channel was the main river. But he wasn't sure it really was the river down here. The river was sweet water but he fished for salt-water prawns in the channel.

'Where does the salt water stop, then?'

'Many miles up. Perhaps towards Hyderabad.' But he had never been there so he wasn't sure.

The geography of the ever-shifting Indus delta was uncertain. The water was brackish, warm and cloudy, neither river nor sea, just a slurry of salt and dirt.

The flow of the Indus has been greatly reduced over the last hundred years by inland irrigation projects. The sea has encroached further and further up the flat delta. Now, the river that in previous centuries was so powerful that it carved a channel in the sea bed, is choked by the sea before it leaves the country.

Further away in the haze I thought I could just glimpse the real ocean, or so I thought from seeing lines of white that might have been waves.

Gani lived in a settlement of three huts. He owned one, his brother owned one and they shared the third. They had ten children each. I sat with him in the shared hut, with its reed walls and raised base designed to let in any passing breeze. The clay here was dry and stamped hard almost to a shine and marked with the concentric circles of salt showing where the sea had evaporated. A few times he described what we could see, fixing me with yellow eyes and speaking slowly and clearly, but at that stage in the trip my Urdu didn't come out smoothly and the oily salt air seemed to be clogging my brain. I nodded and didn't understand. I wondered what I was doing. I had expected the beginning of my journey to be more spectacular.

Gani's mother piled quilts and cushions behind me while we sat. He had invited me to tea but there was some problem with the milk so we just sat together and watched the cushions accumulate behind me.

Gani kept his shrimps in a sliding-topped ice box in one corner of his house. The catch got worse every year as the flow of the Indus reduced and the brackish water suitable for shrimp breeding became increasingly saline. The crab stocks were not so badly affected. It was crab that kept them going. Although very little crab is eaten in Pakistan there is a good export market for it. Boxes of live crabs, cushioned and shaded with leaves, are driven to the airport at Karachi for refrigerated onward travel to Hong Kong and Korea. Gani's morning catch of crabs lay crated beside the ice box, seeping and gurgling like the tidal mudflats that they had come from. Without the crabs, Keti Bandar would have been abandoned long before. Without the town, there would have been no protective dykes and without them there would have been no permanent land. Keti Bandar was really just borrowed from the river for the purpose of supplying shellfish to the restaurants of the East.

'Will you come again?'

'I have much to see, Gani. I must travel the river.'

'When you are finished you must come again. We will eat meat. You are very welcome any time. You are our guest.' I would hear that again and again in Pakistan, the welcome incantation. *Ap hamara mehman hai.* You are our guest.

The engine coughed and died and we drifted down with the current while Gani siphoned the diesel from the makeshift plastic fuel tank. He smiled when the engine started again, yellow eyes and red teeth, and wiped his hands on a much-wiped T-shirt.

'It goes.'

I looked behind me across the wet desert of the delta. By starting at the river's mouth it felt like I was travelling it backwards. At the source it poured out of a glacier bubbling and fresh and cold. Then it gathered strength and watered a whole country. Pakistan without the Indus would be nothing. But down here the river was weak, the creatures that lived in it were transparent and tiny, the men who fished it were yellow and worn out. The river had no energy left and soon it would die. Perhaps it was already dead – there was a sluggish current, but maybe that was like fingernails on a corpse.

Making a journey like this was like writing its biography in reverse, but then, maybe there is nothing wrong with a biography in reverse – you finish with a promise.

It was evening when I caught the pick-up taxi back up the straight road and it was dark while I waited for the bus that would take me back to my hotel at Thatta, the larger stopping-off point for the settlements on the delta. The bus was full and I sat on the roof with forty other men, leaning back on the spare tyre, letting the warm night air blow through my hair, feeling cool at last and more awake than I had felt all day. Now I was moving I felt the excitement – I was at the beginning of something. Anything could happen now.

For the next five months I would always feel a sense of contentment and companionship when I came back to the river. On the roof of that night bus in Sindh, the perforated bowl of the sky above me, I felt that for the first time. I was on a journey to understand the entire life cycle of the Indus, to experience it in all its stages. I had now seen it at its oldest, at its very conclusion. From here, as I travelled upriver, it would get younger every day until I would encounter it at its youngest – at the end of my journey, where it emerged from the ice and was born. While it was dying beneath my boat at Keti Bandar it was being born in Tibet; and when I would see it being born in Tibet it would be dying at the same time.

The bus slowed but didn't stop as I clambered down from the roof in Thatta. It was late and the restaurants had closed so I ate samosas in my room. I washed and lay on the bed and later when I took my clothes off my hands were sticky again from the saltiness that I had carried back with me from the sea.

CHAPTER 2

KARACHI

Sindh and The Punjab both take their names from their rivers. Sindh from the local name for the Indus, Sindhu, and The Punjab from the five tributaries of the Indus that run through the province – *Panj* (Persian for five) and *Ab* (river or water). Were it not for the river and the irrigation system that it now feeds, much of these now heavily populated provinces would have remained a desert.

Not only is the Indus central to sustaining life in these regions, but historians have also argued that the river has played a part in shaping the geopolitics of the lands it flows through. Periods of political disruption have been shown to closely follow periods of disruption caused by the river changing its course or flow rate.[1] The river has also shaped external relations; India's attempt to stem the flow of the Indus tributaries in 1948 was one of several triggers for a worsening of relations between these post-Partition countries.

The river's influence has also stretched into the cultural and spiritual life of the land, feeding the development of religious beliefs and mythology just as it fed the rice paddies and the tall poplar trees whose roots clasped its banks. Indeed, this process came to fascinate me most on my journey – the capacity of the Indus to incubate mythology, the scope for a river to give birth to gods.

The deity of the Sindhi Hindus is Jhulelal, an incarnation of the Hindu river god Varuna. He is depicted as an old man with a long white moustache and beard and he rides the Indus on the back of a pala fish. Jhulelal came to be the Sindhis' god in the tenth century when the territory was home to equal numbers of Hindus and Muslims.

The story goes[2] that the southern Sindhi province of Thatta was ruled by the tyrannical governor, Mirkhshah, who was influenced by a hard-line group of Muslim advisors. One day he called the Hindus of Thatta together and told them they must embrace Islam or die. The Hindus did not know what to do so they all went down to the banks of the Indus and undertook a forty-day vigil in which they prayed daily to Varuna, the water god, and did not shave or use soap to wash. On the fortieth day Varuna spoke to them from the sky and told them that shortly he would take on the physical form of a man and be born from a woman in Nassapur. The Hindus told this to Mirkhshah who agreed to wait and see if their god was coming and delay his promise to kill all those who did not convert to Islam.

Nine months later, as predicted, a boy was born in Nassapur and his birth was accompanied with torrential rains. When the infant opened his mouth his parents saw a vision of the Indus River flowing and an old man with a white beard riding the waves on the back of a pala fish. The boy was christened Uderolal (the one who has come from the water). The cradle that the baby slept in always kept swinging on

---

1 David Oakley, *The Indus River* ed. Azra Meadows and Peter Meadows (Oxford University Press, 1999).

2 The story here is taken from *Sindhi Roots & Rituals Part 2* by Dayal N Harjani (Notion Press, 2018).

its own, like the waves of the Indus; because of this the child was given the nickname Jhulelal, which means 'the swinging child'. Mirkhshah was concerned and attempted to have Jhulelal killed by sending one of his courtiers to visit him with a poisoned rose, but the child frightened the courtier off by morphing into an old man with a white beard and then a warrior with a drawn sword. Mirkhshah decided to wait until the boy grew up and then force his conversion to Islam which would inevitably turn the rest of the Hindus at the same time.

As the boy grew up, he studied under a Vedic scholar and performed the miraculous transformation of beans into rice by casting the jar of beans into the Indus. Mirkhshah finally demanded that he meet Jhulelal who had now become well known in Thatta. The boy was summoned to his court. Mirkhshah told him he must convert along with all the other Hindus of the province. Jhulelal replied,

'Whatever you see around you is the creation of one and only God, whom you call Allah and Hindus call Ishwar. Hindus, Muslims and other human beings are all His creation.'

Mirkhshah laughed at these words and ordered that Jhulelal be arrested and thrown into the stinking prison of Thatta. But as the soldiers advanced on Jhulelal, water ran through the courtyard, flooding the entire palace. At the same time fire broke out and set the whole palace burning. Jhulelal spoke again over the racket of screaming and burning:

'Mirkhshah, think it over again. Your God and mine are not two different ones. Had Almighty so desired, He could have ordained Hindus to be born Muslims. But no; God wanted unity in diversity. The whole world is His manifestation.'

Mirkhshah cried out amidst his flaming, flooding palace,

'I believe you. I realise the truth now.'

Mirkhshah bowed to Jhulelal and agreed to treat Hindus and Muslims alike. The persecution of Hindus stopped and a temple was built in Thatta to Jhulelal. Jhulelal now travelled around Sindh preaching and establishing temples. At Halla, his temple was built in fields belonging to a Muslim man and despite his religion this man and his wife became its caretakers. This temple became a pilgrimage site for Hindus and Muslims. Jhulelal travelled as far up the river as Rohri where there is a ghat named after him. His miracles and philosophy made him hugely popular among Hindus and Muslims throughout Sindh.

When he reached the age of thirteen Jhulelal realised that the purpose for which he had come to earth was over. He returned to his birthplace and prepared to die. Crowds of followers gathered, including his devotees and representatives of Mirkhshah. When he died, the Hindus said they would build a *samadhi*, a Hindu shrine, devoted to him. The Muslims disagreed and said that they would build a *turbat*, a Muslim shrine, according to their religion. While this debate was going on heavy rain started pouring from the sky and a voice from the heavens said:

'Make my shrine acceptable to both Hindus and Muslims. Let its one part be like a Hindu temple and the other part be like a Muslim shrine. I BELONG TO ALL OF YOU.' And so the building was made on the site of his death, with one door being the entrance of the *turbat*, the Muslim shrine, and the other door being the entrance of the *samadhi*, the Hindu temple.

I liked this medieval story of Jhulelal. While he is most closely connected to Sindh province, he appears in Hindu temples in Gujarat and other north Indian states, particularly in areas where Sindhi Hindu exiles settled after Partition. Whenever I saw his image in temples in India I always made a point of leaving rupees for him.

Normally it was on a side shrine, subordinate to the popular gods. But he was always recognisable, looking dignified and regal with his turban and neat white beard (he was always shown as the wise old man that he transformed himself into rather than as the boy that he was), and beneath his crossed legs the bemused-looking pala fish. I liked him because of his connections with the river that I would grow close to, but I liked him also because he was a unifier.

While Sindh has the highest proportion of Hindus in any province of Pakistan, they still make up a small minority. On Partition millions of Hindus left Sindh for India and a similar number of Muslims arrived in Pakistan from India, many of them heading for Karachi. Hindus now make up less than eight per cent of the Sindh population, but as I travelled through the province I found echoes of what Hinduism had left behind. Jhulelal's image was now rarely to be found in post-Partition Sindh but in some ways his ecumenical influence was still strong.

From the delta town of Thatta I travelled back to the sprawling coastal metropolis of Karachi and one evening I took the bus to the upmarket suburb of Clifton, up the road from the first McDonald's in Pakistan. There, near the beach, is the shrine of Abdullah Shah Ghazi. I walked through *Funland* to get there, past the go-kart track where the children of rich Cliftonites ran one another over, and the Chinese circus tent which pulled in the punters by putting a hula-hooping girl in a short pink dress on show outside.

The shrine was perched on a rocky hill looking out towards the sea. There are conflicting stories about the saint's background. Some say he was a trader from Medina in the Arabian Peninsula, others that the shrine covers the tomb of an Umayyad general. The saint is said to have particularly strong links to the sea. Fishermen come to pray for calm seas, Karachiites believe his shrine protects the city from cyclones and by some accounts, his arrival in Sindh was a result of him being the only survivor of a shipwreck off the coast.

The crowds moved in a one-way flow up the stairs and through the perfumed atria, then squeezed into the narrow passage around the raised sarcophagus. The white marble steps were draped with embroidered green velvet and strewn with petals and devotional sweets.

The pilgrims muttered prayers then touched the drapes with their hands and drew their hands over their faces. *Bismillah* they whispered, the word drawn out like poetry or a spell, *BISsss-millaaah*. Some of them pulled the velvet over their heads, absorbing the blessings through their scalps and hissing their prayers urgently at the stone, as if this saint might take some persuading or cajoling. In the corner stood a Sufi ascetic who to me looked indistinguishable from a Hindu sadhu. He wore a black tunic and a broad necklace made from rows of jangling metal links. Slung over his back was a long wooden bow made from black wood and a matching black quiver of arrows. In his hand was a black wooden staff that curled and twisted to a gnarled end well above his head. The dress was theatrical; he looked like a mythological hunter. But beneath the outfit his body was old and slight. His hair was white like his beard and his eyes were lined and deep set in wrinkled craters. He wore the classic Sindhi hat, a brightly coloured skullcap, inset with mirrors, with the fabric cut and hemmed to create an arch shape over the forehead. It was the only piece of his clothing that wasn't black. As I watched him he unhooked a horn from his belt, made from the same black wood as his bow, and blew two blasts on it that caused everyone momentarily to pause and look at him. He cried something in a strangled high voice, and the visitors shouted back, '*Wah, Allah*'. Then he was quiet again. He stood alone, like a sentry, and when pilgrims approached him it was to hand him a few rupees, wordlessly. I had seen lines of figures just like him among the Hindu sadhus in Varanasi who called themselves the *Naga Babs*. They were symbolic warriors too; they arranged themselves in regiments and called themselves the warriors of Shiva.

The saint's shrine rose out of a tooth of rock. To one side the rock had been extended with concrete which sprouted concrete reinforcing poles. Back down the sun-warmed steps a path led to a cave and the freshwater spring that legend has it the saint first brought to life. The water formed a pool in the shadowy grotto beneath the rock. Devotees believed that the saint's curative powers were transmitted through the water, and families clustered around the pipes that led from the pool drinking beaker after beaker of it and sprinkling it over their children. Beside the pool sat another holy man. This one was also bound in chains and sat staring in front of him. One of the men drinking from the spring approached me as I was looking at the holy man.

'Thirty kay-jees of steel. Pure steel. Pure holy man.' I never saw ascetics like this in the city mosques of Pakistan and certainly not in the many (often Saudi-funded) Wahhabi mosques that dot the countryside, but in the Sufi saints' shrines these theatrical characters were tolerated and even celebrated.

As twilight approached, the shrine was lit up with bulbs and fairy lights and the families disappeared. The evening visitors were younger men from the city, who milled about the dusty area beneath the shrine, or gathered in groups and sat along the sloping side of the rock making the air sweet with marijuana smoke. Cold drink carts rolled in, lit up in colours and blaring music, '*gala thanda, gala thanda*'.

The only light came from their flashing lights, the strings of bulbs on the bunting and the glowing white dome of the shrine above us.

When it got dark the dancing began.

The musicians stood in groups and pounded the taut skins of their double-sided dhols, a type of drum widespread in the subcontinent. Men crowded round them and sometimes adolescent boys broke into a gap at the centre, dancing with their hands above their heads, looking over their shoulders suggestively. Some of the men gave the boys money. Then they joined them, pointing at the sky with both their forefingers and treading the ground, sending dust into the air with each step until it looked like they were smouldering.

I moved from group to group among the close-packed throngs of spectators. The crowds grew until I was crushed in the jostling warmth of hundreds of bodies, the air filled with the smoke of tobacco and hashish and the smell of betel and dust.

In the midst of the beating drums and the strange pungent smells I heard a familiar sound. Beside the drummers a tall man swung the drones of a set of bagpipes on to his shoulders and began to tune them. He struck the chanter in, and it protested and squealed while he twisted it round to his fingers. Then he played a tune that was quite different from anything I have heard on the pipes before. The same phrase came over and over again, sliding up and down the scale. It used the same grace notes, the taorluaths, the birls that I had been taught a decade before by my bagpipe teacher at school, but the chanter was different – it sang the oriental scale with the tone that made me think of snake charmers. Everything else was the same, however: sterling silver mouthpiece, tartan bag, braided cords between the drones. I watched the group dance to his music for a long time, waiting for him to finish. I wanted to find out where he had learned to play this instrument and what these strange foreign tunes were called. But the dancers kept stuffing rupees into his pocket so he carried on going until thirst drove me away to the *gala thanda* carts.

I drank pomegranate juice with shaved ice. By this time there were burger trolleys there too, radiating more heat from their huge smoking griddles. People jostled each other, shouting and laughing, weaving between the refreshments and the musicians. They did not seem to be particularly pious pilgrims. I imagined the reality was that these men were Karachi bachelors (or escaping husbands) who came to the dusty field by Abdullah Shah Ghazi's shrine to cut loose. They came to get stoned and dance.

I spent several weeks travelling around Sindh, criss-crossing the flood plain of the Indus, and it was always the Sufi shrines of dead saints that drew me in. Particularly striking was the shrine of Manghopir, to the north of Karachi, situated in the midst of a community of black Pakistanis. These people, called the Sheedis, are said to be the descendants of slaves brought centuries earlier along the trade routes from Africa.

Whenever I asked Karachiites about the black Pakistanis they always said the blacks were dirty. In the fish market they were the ones who carried the loaded baskets on their heads so their clothes were soaked with ice melt and covered in fish scales. They were looked down upon and seemed a marginalised group. Their jobs made them dirty, but at the Manghopir shrine they looked quite the opposite.

The men wore pristine *shalwar kameez* not in the drab, traditional colours but in strawberry pink, red and violet. The women's headscarves flashed patterns and in the dazzling light I could see through their gauzy folds to the curves of their long necks. Some of them looked completely African but others were mixed so that the curls in their hair tumbled and their noses were neither flattened nor pointed.

Pir Mangho, or Sheikh Hafiz Haji Hasan-al-Maroof Sultan Manghopir, to give him his full name, was a holy man who came from Arabia to Sindh in the thirteenth century. Manghopir has been adopted by the Sheedis as their shrine. A large community of them live nearby but others come from far away, to visit the resting place of the saint who also came from far across the water.

Like Abdullah Shah Ghazi's, Pir Mangho's shrine was marked by water, with miraculous cures delivered through the medium of a spring. In the parched desert of Sindh it is unsurprising that a spring should be associated with something miraculous and holy. But this idea of sacred places being marked by pools of water had hints of Hinduism to it too; bathing is an important ritualised process in Hindu holy places. Here at Manghopir, next to the warm, sulphurous springs capable of curing the rheumatics who bathed in them, was a larger marshy pool walled in with spiked railings. Basking on the banks or motionless in the water like floating logs were forty snub-nosed crocodiles.

The legend goes that these crocodiles grew from the head lice that Pir Mangho combed from his head after stepping off the boat from Arabia. The truth is that these were probably Indus River crocodiles stranded in their marshy lake when the river changed course. Children threw popcorn at them and it bounced off their armour or stuck to the mud that oozed between their long claws. Some visitors came with offerings and when they tossed the slabs of fresh meat into the pool the crocodiles thrashed and showed their teeth and slapped the meat against the water as if to kill it. Then they tossed it backwards along their long jaws and swallowed it whole.

I kept on having to remind myself – all this is Islam. While I knew that the Islam of Pakistan was a more inclusive, localised religion than the Wahhabi version of Saudi Arabia, it still fascinated me to see the traces of older religions in the shrines around Sindh. But new religions in all countries are built on the foundations of old; the influences of the old seep through and are assimilated, creating syncretic sites and festivals. When a new religion arrives it takes up residence in the halls of its predecessor. Sometimes the same furniture remains in use, and it only takes a little scraping of the varnish to see that the shadows of the old gods live on. In Sindh this adoption was particularly strong, demonstrated so clearly in Lord Jhulelal's two-doored shrine.

While these shrines suggested tolerance and the memory of overlapping religions, in other ways Sindh was scarred with divisions. The day before I arrived a bomb went off in a Karachi mosque, killing 14 people. It was a Shia mosque, so Karachi Shias were out in force stoning police vans, smashing up Sunni shops and shouting for revenge. Police in grey-and-blue camouflage – designed more to inspire fear than to conceal the city's paramilitary force, it seemed – patrolled the streets all day and the shops didn't open. I kept to my hotel room for a day watching the news.

BBC World News aired a repeating loop of speeding ambulances and heaps of rubble. The bomber, they said, had been dressed as a Shia cleric. The real cleric who had been leading the prayers had been killed. Distant shots revealed smoke rising around the domed building. Pakistan TV (PTV) showed the mosque interior: howling bodies in the hammocks of blanket stretchers, and the high domed ceiling stained with broad splashes of red. It looked like the corridor of my hotel where years of guests spitting out their betel nut paan against the wall had left layers of watery red stains. The news coverage was gruesome and relentless and soon I could take no more and switched it off.

Riots and unrest are a frequent feature of the uncontrolled sprawl of Pakistan's largest city. Poverty and a high proportion of migrancy exacerbates friction among a population whose main problem is that it can be cut so many different ways. There is the potential for ethnic divisions between all the regional groups of immigrants, in particular the Sindhi Karachiites and Mohajirs (Muslim incomers who arrived from India following Partition). But currently worse than this is the sectarian divide between the two great strands of Islam, the Sunnis and Shias.

Riots soon followed the bomb. Fifty people were arrested. One was killed. There was tear gas. All this happened in the city centre but all I could hear was that the street was quieter because when there was trouble people knew it was better to stay inside. Three weeks later a Sunni cleric was assassinated in a revenge attack. The following week there was a bomb in the Shia mosque closest to where the assassination had taken place. Karachi's cycles of violence spun on. PTV showed more riots, and for a few more days Karachi's street life was hushed. Then things went back to normal and Karachi forgot its troubles as it has learned to do. The cobbler set out his flaps of leather around a telephone pole, the mango carts rolled out again and the poster seller displayed his political kitsch on a wider bit of pavement – Osama Bin Laden on a white horse, Saddam Hussein with an RPG launcher, a neon-coloured panorama of Mecca.

I left Karachi and went north, keen to get away from the bombs and tear gas towards more shrines where religious lines were blurred and where gods lived in the river.

CHAPTER 3

BHIT SHAH AND
LAKE MANCHAR

In Sindh, as I made my way north from Karachi up the east bank of the Indus, my journey was measured in shrines. In my own way I became a shrine devotee, seeking out the curved domes on the skyline and detouring away from the main road to tiny villages where saints had expired centuries before. Thursday night is the night of activity at Sufi shrines, the night before the day of prayers. I always tried to make sure I was near an interesting shrine on a Thursday.

Bhit Shah is the shrine of one of Pakistan's most famous poets, Shah Abdul Latif. A man approached me as I sat beneath a tree in the courtyard sketching the saint's mausoleum, and spoke in English.

'I was told there was a foreigner visiting today but I did not recognise you. You look like a Pakistani. Where are you from? Would you mind if I talked to you?' He crouched as he talked, bringing his face level with mine and tilting his head deferentially. When I nodded he sat down beside me and introduced himself as Nadir. We talked in the shade of the neem tree while the Thursday afternoon pilgrims milled around us.

Nadir was a follower of the philosophy of Shah Abdul Latif. He was originally from Balochistan but had travelled to this religious centre to study. Now I noticed the Balochi looks that set him apart from the Sindhis. He had paler skin, wiry hair and narrow eyes that seemed to be constantly squinting at the sun.

He had the dishevelled appearance of academics who are overly focused on their studies. His cream shalwar kameez had the shadowy grey creases that suggested a few days' wear, and there was a button missing from one of his cuffs. As he talked his nervous fingers switched between holding closed his button-less cuff and rotating the turquoise set ring that he wore on his middle finger.

He told me how, when the saint came to this place for the first time in the early eighteenth century, he sat meditating on a sand hill, or *bhit*, for three years. How after that he had built the village with his bare hands. How he composed poetry in Sindhi, Balochi and Pashtun but could only write one letter of the Arabic alphabet, the first one, the Alif. How his devotion to the ascetic life had persuaded him to use his powers to make his wife miscarry so that he would not be tied to the world with children but how he had made another woman pregnant just by touching the saliva of his tongue to hers. How he had sat for years with his legs crossed but with his knees pointing up because he was so devoted an ascetic that he wanted to use up as little space on the ground as possible.

Nadir explained this complex saint to me in English saying each sentence in three different ways, using different words or pronouncing each one differently. His vocabulary was complex and his use of tenses conscientious. But the strain of speaking in a foreign language seemed to affect his short-term memory so that he would forget where he was in a story and revert to something that he had already said. The story about sitting on the sand hill seemed to be a favourite. It was like speaking to a stutterer. At each pause, his mouth quivered as his lips formed a foreign shape and in the delay I wanted to prompt him. When I tried to speak to him in Urdu he smiled as if this was a bit of a joke, something that was rather sweet of me to try but not really worth pursuing.

'I will speak English. Don't worry.'

I noticed that while we talked, Nadir sat with his arms around his knees, by habit imitating the space-saving pose of the saint. He called over to a teenaged boy, the brother of a friend, to bring drinks to us. The boy had been working on the fabric of the shrine and carried his tools – a saw, a hammer and a chisel – bunched in his hand like a guild representative from a medieval woodcut. He brought us a jug of water-buffalo milk floating with a fist-sized block of ice.

'You like milk?', the boy asked. 'It is the milk of my water buffalo. How many water buffalo does your family own?'

'None, I'm afraid.'

He looked sympathetic. 'It does not matter.'

Nadir talked on. Shah Abdul Latif still confused him. Some things the saint said were incomprehensible to him. He fixed me with his sun-creased eyes, and his fingernails made tiny taps as they pushed the turquoise ring faster round his finger.

'Once he praised prostitutes over respectable women.' That was the most I could gather from that tale. Each line of the story was repeated in so many different ways that it lacked any coherence. He spoke with the pondering confusion of an academic confronted with a great philosophical contradiction. I tried to hurry him along but Nadir didn't like being interrupted.

As the afternoon wore on Nadir's friends came to talk to us. They were similar in character to Nadir, reserved and pensive. Shah Abdul

Latif was what bound them; in their free time they took it in turns to work at the shrine teahouse and they could sit for hours and talk about their saint.

He introduced me to someone he claimed was a descendant of the Abdul Latif family.

'This man is great-great-great- and ten more greats grandson of Shah Abdul Latif. Maybe more greats. We are not sure.' The man smiled, lips pulled back from his teeth as if posing for a photo. He had floppy gelled hair and a jet-black shalwar kameez. The others made space for him and he lounged on the charpoy, smoking and slurping tea. I thought of his ancestor sitting on the sand hill using as little space as possible. He asked me questions and laughed at my Urdu, repeating it back to me in an exaggerated way. He was different from Nadir's other friends. He didn't join in the conversations about the saint – he looked bored and tried to change the subject. Mostly they indulged this holy descendant and tried to laugh when he said something apparently amusing but Nadir became agitated and made an excuse for us to sit on another charpoy.

'I am sorry. He is uneducated, that is not good. I am sorry that he talks to you in this way. What can I say?' Nadir felt awkward that I was the joke. But later when the descendant came over to us as he was leaving, Nadir shook his hand. He did it solemnly and warmly and I could see that he was shaking hands with the family line of Shah Abdul Latif, not the slightly rude man that this descendant happened to be.

Settling as the saint did so close to the Indus, it is unsurprising that the river is a recurring feature in his work. Often it was the setting for his love stories, for Shah Abdul Latif was a prolific storyteller. Two of his most famous stories are centred on the flow of the waters. In the story of Suhni and Mehar, the beautiful Mehar swims across the Indus every night to visit her illicit lover Suhni, who is a buffalo herder. She uses a clay pot as a float. One night her jealous sister-in-law swaps the pot for one of unbaked clay which causes her to drown. Her lover Suhni drowns in a whirlpool while trying to save her.

In the story of Sassi and Pannu, a Hindu Brahmin sees in a vision that his daughter will marry a Muslim. Seeking to avoid this he puts the baby girl in a box and floats her down the river. She ends up in a family of poor clothes-washers until a passing prince falls in love with her. The two are separated and eventually die trying to reunite in the middle of the Thar Desert.

Later in Lahore I bought a miniature painting of the lovers riding on camels across the desert. They had originally been painted on the same sheet of paper – the borders' patterns lined up – but they had been cut in two and framed separately so that on my wall they continually chase each other across the desert, forever separated by their frames.

In the evening, music began inside the shrine. Five men in black shalwar kameez sat on cushions in a semicircle with their tambours resting on their crossed legs.

They sang slowly at first. A single note in almost unison. Then the octave above. They took it in turns to sing – a male chest voice then falsetto. The music sped up and the players beat the wood of their tambours as they plucked the strings, bringing in percussion with the two notes.

Nadir leaned closer. 'There are thirty-six styles in which they will sing Shah Abdul Latif's poetry. They will go on until the morning.'

A shriek came from where the women sat, separated from men on the other side of the courtyard, and one of them began swinging her head round, slapping the marble floor with the flat of her hand. Her hair came free of her scarf and flew round as she lurched with the rhythm of the tambour. 'A fairy has taken hold of her mind,' Nadir explained. 'It is not her that is dancing but something like a fairy has come into her with the music and is making her move. It is infuriating her.'

But apart from the lone possessed woman, the audience was quiet and contemplative, sitting cross-legged in the cool forest of pillars.

After two or three varieties of verse we went to one of the kitchens outside the shrine and as we scooped up dal with pinches of roti, Nadir asked me where I was going. I told him that next on my list was the shrine of Qalandar Shah in Sehwan and that I intended to visit the fishing tribe called the Mohana who have lived on a nearby lake for generations.

'Shah Abdul Latif wrote a story about the Mohana. I would love to see these things.'

I wondered if he would travel with me. He would be a good companion. As a scholar and an incomer to Sindh the things that interested him often interested me too. One of the benefits of making a journey alone is that it enables you to travel with lots of different people.

'You should come along with me.' I suggested.

Nadir smiled and looked at the curved tiles on the roof then down at his hands. The ring twisted round his finger. I wondered if he was thinking of a good excuse not to come or if he worried that I had only offered out of politeness. The decision seemed to make him nervous. Perhaps he felt duty-bound to accompany me or perhaps he felt he would be an imposition.

I filled the silence. 'Perhaps you don't have time, you have duties, but it would be no trouble…'

But he broke in with a surprising earnestness. 'I will come to Sehwan with you. I would like to go.'

I half expected not to see him at the bus stop the next morning. I thought he might have reconsidered or forgotten overnight, but he arrived in time. He had brought no luggage with him, just a parcel of chapatti which we chewed on in the bus, as he told me the story that Shah Abdul Latif had written about the Mohana.

'There is a tribe called the Mohana people who live on the lakes and the rivers of Sindh. They cannot live in houses for it is not their custom and instead they live on houseboats called *doondis* and they work in smaller boats using *katra* nets to fish the Sindhi waterways. Because they are living by catching and selling fish, they were always smelling of fish. The men work outdoors all day in the baking heat of the sun which turns their skin black and they are always poor and hungry so they do not grow tall like their neighbours on the land. The women grow old quickly, they are ugly and they smell of fish. In the towns when they come to sell their catch, people avoid them because they are not nice to look at and their smell is strong. This is how they know they are Mohana.

'But one day a Mohana girl was born and she is called Noori. As soon as she is born they can tell that she is different. She is the most beautiful girl and although she works like the Mohana have always worked, with the fish, she never smells of fish. Not at all. Instead she smells sweet, like rose water or sandalwood soap.

'The prince of that part of Sindh was named Jam Tamachi and he saw Noori while he was sailing on Kinjhar Lake and he fell in love with her. When he told his men that he would marry Noori they laughed because she was a Mohana and everyone knew that the Mohana were the ugliest, smelliest people in the whole world. But he brought her to his palace and when they saw her they understood how he could fall in love with her because she was the most beautiful girl that they had ever seen. In those days the princes had many different wives but there was always one wife who was the first wife, and she would be the favourite of the Prince. Jam Tamachi was a big prince and had many, many beautiful wives and he found it difficult to decide who should be the chief wife.

'One night he held a competition to help him decide. He told all his wives to be beautiful because that night he would choose his chief wife. All of the wives dressed up in their best clothes and covered themselves with jewels, all except Noori. Noori stayed in her simple clothes made of plain cloth but when they walked before Jam Tamachi, she was the most beautiful of them all. Jam Tamachi chose her to be his boss-in-charge wife, and to reward the Mohana tribe for providing him with his favourite he made a gift of the lake waters of the Sindh to them forever and he made a law that they would never pay tax again.

'It is because of this that Jam Tamachi is called the "father of fishermen" and it is because of this that his tomb stands on a tiny island in Kinjhar Lake, on the spot where he first saw Noori. That is the story of the Mohana.'

I thanked Nadir for telling the story. 'We should look out for pretty girls at Lake Manchar?' I joked.

'No. It is a story. The Mohana are not clean people and not beautiful people.'

We rode on in silence. The Sindhi desert spread on either side of the road, vast and unchanging. The bus windows were blue, so when I got off at the stops to stretch my legs the desert appeared to be a Martian red for a minute or two until my eyes adjusted. Schoolchildren got on in a cluster of blue and white and screamed at the conductor to blow his whistle so that the driver would stop and let them off outside their houses. A long-eared goat knelt in the central aisle chewing a mango-flavoured straw from a juice carton.

Lake Manchar is fed from the Kirthar hills to the west and acts as a safety valve for the Indus, taking massive inflows when the river floods and draining it back out again in the low season. We arrived during the morning fish market. The fish were plump and silver-scaled and they were laid out on chipped ice.

Gulam, one of the fishermen, offered to take us out in his boat. Nadir was nervous when I suggested we go.

'It is dangerous, the boats are small. I will not go.' He shook his head and went to sit in the teahouse, so I went out alone with Gulam on the lake.

The lake edge was an extension of the playground between the huts and the village children lived like amphibians, always wet. The young girls swam around the boat in dresses, their long braided hair held in their mouths. As we poled away from the shore, naked boys with stick legs ran along the sand spit islands, keeping up with us, waving or walking along underwater shoals. When they could go no further they stopped and waved at us until their shouts were faint. On our way back they were still there, picking molluscs from the mud.

Further out we passed moored houseboats, the *doondis*, wide high-bowed craft, each one sending up a vertical line of smoke from the on-board cooking fire. It was nearly midday and stiflingly hot so we beached the boat on a reed-covered sandbank and waded into the lake to cool off. I swam away from the reeds but the water stayed shallow and when I put my feet down I felt the bottom, soft mud hiding hard sticks and things that slithered.

Early travellers up the Indus wrote about the Mohanas' unique river-fishing method. This involved driving the fish into bottlenecks of pitched nets. With nowhere else to go the fish would jump over the netted end, conveniently landing themselves in waiting baskets. It sounded a marvellously satisfying way of fishing. However, on Lake Manchar now they used homemade fine nylon mesh nets which they spread across the deeper channels, buoyed with blocks of polystyrene.

We hailed one of the boats and Gulam pointed out the different kinds of fish: morakhee, a wide, yellow, carp-like fish, each scale traced with grey edges, and suhnee, little oval fish with outsized eyes. I bought one of the morakhee and Gulam gutted it with his fingers, wrapped it in a wet cloth and put it in the shadows of the bow.

Others fished between the islands with casting nets. One stood on the bow, thin legs appearing from a sun-bleached *lunghi*. Sweat ran from his thick hair which he had grown over his eyes to protect them from the glare. He scooped old dal into an arc over the water to attract the fish, then flung out the pleated net so that its lead-weighted edges tightened into a circle as it landed. He let it sink then pulled the rope that tightened the draw-cord and steadily brought the net back to the boat. He killed the twitching patches of silver in his net by driving a spike in above their eyes so that they couldn't flip back into the water.

Back at the shore Gulam's wife cooked the fish. Their house was busy with his extended family: one aunt beat the washing on the semi-curve of an old concrete pipe, young girls wandered the shore with babies propped on their hips and watched me closely, a brother cut new polystyrene floats from the moulded shapes of TV packaging, grandma emerged from the dark interior, stick thin and hollow cheeked, cackling at the joke of me sitting on the charpoy, then settled down to weave nets from green nylon thread. To help her concentrate she smoked what looked like blackened plant stems in the bowl of a pottery hookah.

When the fish was cooked the whole family gathered round a tablecloth laid on palm mats and pulled pieces from the plate. It was delicious; white and flaky like plaice, in a rich masala with potatoes and chilli. I scooped it up with a chapatti brushed with ghee.

After lunch Gulam took me up to his other house, built on an artificial embankment away from the flood plain of the lake. It was very smart. Metal plates were arranged in a cabinet like the china in a Victorian parlour. The charpoys here were covered in blankets and cushions, and inside the thick mud-brick walls the air was pleasantly cool. The government had gifted a house like this to each of the Mohana families around the lake but Gulam's family only stayed here when the water was too high; otherwise they preferred to be down on the shore.

'We used to live in houseboats when the water went high but the government bought my boat and gave us the house.'

The Sindh provincial government has been trying to move the Mohana on to dry land since the 1970s. The reduction in the river's flow caused by barrages and canals brought about increasing pollution and this is gradually reducing the fish yield and the livelihood of the

Mohana. Their exclusive right to fish the river and lakes (granted by the starry-eyed Jam Tamachi) was removed in 1947 and more efficient fishing boats have starting competing with the Mohana. Their gypsy life on the lakes and rivers has become increasingly poor and the government's response has been to encourage them to settle on land where they can make a better living. However, this project has largely failed because the Mohana have been reluctant to leave their water homes or unable to adapt to the new skills of farming.

'Tell me about the Mohana who moved away,' I asked. But the question didn't interest Gulam.

'Some people moved.' He had nothing more to say.

'They say the fishing is more difficult now.'

'There are still fish. You saw them. There are always fish in the water.'

The reality is that there are fewer and fewer, but Gulam would not talk about it.

Reading about the Mohana, I had come across something else which fascinated me. There was another water-dwelling tribe who lived alongside them. These non-Muslim people, called the Jabbahs, lived by hunting the Indus dolphin, a blind dolphin similar to the blind Ganges dolphin, both of which are now protected species. I wondered what had become of the Jabbahs now that they could no longer trap the dolphins. But Gulam laughed at me when I asked and said he didn't know, he had never heard of the Jabbahs and he didn't know anyone who fished for dolphins.

'In January we will circumcise my son.' He pointed to the naked boy beside us who, as if he understood what had been said, ran to hide behind his grandma. The boy jumped up and down half hidden and laughed as he saw his father laugh. Then he ran off to the lake and leapt in, seeking comfort in the constant of his watery playground.

It was still by the lake and as the sun grew stronger its glare was mirrored back at the land. The shore was quiet as the families retreated into the shade of their huts to sit out the hottest hours. The amphibious children didn't seem to notice, though, and continued splashing around on the sand spits. Nadir and I took the bus back to Sehwan. The curtains on the bus windows flapped and let in choking gusts of hot wind like the exhaust from heavy machinery. When I held my scarf across my face my hands burned in the heat and my fingernails hurt as though they were resting on a radiator. All the passengers tied scarves around their heads, leaving only a slit to see through so we looked like a bus of guerrilla fighters.

Back in the hotel I lay and sweated. The lazy fan wafted warm air around the room. I drank a whole bottle of water and still my urine was a worrying deep orange. I drank another and longed for evening.

I was ill the next day and lay panting and shuttling between damp bed and bathroom. Nadir politely retreated outside and left me alone. In the afternoon I crept out to buy water and a copy of *Dawn*, an English-language Pakistani newspaper, where I read about the ongoing problem of pollution in Lake Manchar. Several people had died in Hyderabad and Karachi following the release of toxic water from the lake into the supply reservoirs. While my guts twisted around themselves I read an article titled *The Killer Lake*, with the strap line *The entire ecosystem of Manchar Lake has been severely disturbed by effluents.* At the time it seemed reasonable to assume that since I had eaten Manchar fish and swum in Manchar waters the day before I was a victim of this outflow, although I was probably just suffering from a routine stomach upset.

Manchar's problems stemmed from Pakistan's eternal problem of not having enough water. All through The Punjab and Sindh the Indus was sucked at by canals and held up by barrages to serve a rapidly growing population. Lake Manchar is constantly polluted by chemicals, sewage and hyper-saline streams and the Indus has now become too weak to flush it out annually, as it used to. The pollutants collect in the lake and slowly kill it. In 1950 the fish catch of Manchar was 3,000 tonnes per year, in the mid-1990s it was 300 tonnes, now it is just a few tonnes per year and, the article added, 'the colour of fish is also black and the quality poor.' (Although the fish I ate may have made me ill, I couldn't remember anything wrong with its colour or taste.) The article continued, 'most fishermen have migrated elsewhere, to meet their economic needs.'

I thought back to my conversation with Gulam. Surely, working so closely with the lake, he must have noticed the dwindling stocks and the change in the fish. But he had said nothing about it. Maybe he didn't want to talk about these problems with a stranger; that was one explanation. But another was that he didn't even want to think about it. The very self-image of the Mohana was built on the fact that they lived off the water; this was one of the reasons it was so difficult to settle them on the land. The possibility that the water might not be supporting them, that their world was dying, was a frightening one. The Mohana who left the dying lake were perhaps best forgotten or not talked about because they were the proof that the lake could no longer sustain them.

I thought back to the story of Prince Jam Tamachi and Noori and what he had given her people. With the birth of Pakistan the Mohana lost their exclusive right to fish the lakes. And now the lakes had turned sour.

CHAPTER 4

MOHENJO DARO

Mohenjo Daro is one of the largest settlements of the Indus Valley Civilisation, one of the three earliest civilisations on earth. It was built in 2500BCE and, after its decline in the nineteenth century BCE, lay under dust and river sediment for thousands of years until it was rediscovered in the 1920s by the Archaeological Survey of India.

I arrived at the archaeological site in the evening as the heat was dying. Goat bells sounded from the surrounding fields and the buffalo complained as they were herded towards the milking sheds. The plants that had hung dusty and lifeless during the day gave off relieved green breaths when the sun set. It felt strange that people and animals came alive as the sun died. During the day, the sun had the effect of freezing life as it rose in the sky. Animals didn't even eat in the midday sun, they just stood by the trees or found pools of water to wallow in. My friends in the north had laughed when I told them I was going to visit Sindh in June. 'The heat will kill you,' they said. 'You should not go south in June.' Each day on the baked, white plains I remembered this – but I had no choice. Sindh would not be pleasant again until November and I had to return home in October.

Akbar, the museum curator, met me and helped me get a room at the archaeological dak-bungalow, the official rest house for visiting workers. No archaeology is undertaken in the hot season so I was the only one staying there. In the morning I had to tell the cook what I wanted for dinner and he would serve it to me alone at a long Formica table in the dining room.

I stayed at the site for three days. In the mornings and the evenings, when it was possible to walk outside, I paced the dusty streets of the excavated city and for the rest of the time I read on the shaded benches of the veranda. Around midday, when the intensity of the light seemed to send the air humming as if an electrical charge was running through it, I went to talk to Akbar. His office had a window-mounted water cooler – a sort of rudimentary air conditioner that blew air through moist straw. We talked about his theories on the civilisation and I browsed the hundreds of volumes of the green leather-bound journal *Pakistan Archaeology* while I sat in an armchair and enjoyed the damp rushing air.

The ruins of Mohenjo Daro spread around the dak-bungalow in a sea of beige right angles. The only thing that stuck out of this dusty brick maze was a large stupa, but this later Buddhist addition that used scavenged Indus Valley bricks was nothing to do with the original civilisation. The rest of the site is remarkable only in its uniformity and regularity. Unlike the civilisations of Mesopotamia and Dynastic Egypt that scholars of the Indus Valley claim emerged slightly later, there are no signs of Indus Valley kingship or hierarchical power. Mohenjo Daro did appear to have a form of religion that required special if not particularly impressive structures. What emerges most clearly from the design of the city is a clear veneration of water.

One of the few unusual structures in the city is the ceremonial bath. This is shaped like a small rectangular swimming pool, built from high-quality fired bricks and waterproofed with tar. The quality of the workmanship and the size relative to the city suggests its ceremonial rather than recreational purpose. The importance of water is also evident in the sophisticated drainage system, using brick channels covered by regularly cut flat stones. The system incorporates the earliest known examples of public toilets, with sewage carefully separated from freshwater channels. The system of wells is extensive, with one well for every three houses; a provision of water that seems far beyond that required by necessity. The wells are carefully constructed using wedge-shaped, kiln-fired bricks. The same bricks are used for the bathing platforms that are found in most houses, and it is evident from the contents of the drains that bathing involved the ritual or practical use of clay triangles as skin scrubbers or a substitute for toilet paper. In addition to an over-provision of wells, many of the houses also have external cisterns, which appear to have been used to collect waste water. There is a clear emphasis on the importance of clean water from the wells, and a suggestion from the complex provisions for waste water that there was something ceremonial about it – that the water was dirty in more than the purely practical sense. Modern-day archaeologists have called this preoccupation with water in the Indus Valley Civilisation *wasserluxus.*

In the heat of Sindh I could easily understand the importance placed on water. I had developed my own midday bathing rituals. I would sluice myself with water from the bucket shower and stand naked under the ceiling fan. It was the only time of day when I wasn't sweating. At night I slept under wet towels like a fever patient.

But there was more to the Indus Valley Civilisation's *wasserluxus* than the soothing effects of water. Mohenjo Daro worshipped with water because this was a civilisation that was, quite simply, Indus obsessed. The broad river that ran alongside the city was vital to the city's prosperity. It brought in merchants in their high-prowed *doondi* boats, and a healthy trade with Egypt and Mesopotamia. Cotton as a commodity was probably first cultivated in the Indus Valley, and the Egyptian Pharaoh's linen gown was made from Indus cotton. The Indus fertilised the surrounding farmland with the rich alluvial silt that washed over it during the perennial flooding.

Clay seals show the boats and wagons that brought trading goods to Mohenjo Daro. Other seals show the importance of natural forces to the fertility of the Indus farmland. In one of these seals a horned bull is shown ravaging a female figure who lies flat on the ground. The brutality of the act is unmistakable and yet as a result of this ravaging, the female figure is sprouting a plant from her torso. The message would appear to be that from the aggression and pain imposed by natural forces the female Mother Earth is made fertile. We know that the Indus was destructive in this area because Mohenjo Daro is built on top of a manmade mound of rubble and brick chippings, a hugely time-consuming precaution which must have been necessary to protect this important administrative centre from the flood plain.

Although Hinduism did not exist at the time of the Indus Valley people, the idea that creation must be preceded by destruction has similarities with Hindu beliefs. The Hindu sacred text, the *Rig Veda*, suggests the creation of the universe might have been the result of a sacrifice, with the quartering of a human figure preceding creation:

Forth from his navel came mid-air; the sky was fashioned from his head; Earth from his feet, and from his ear the regions. Thus they formed the worlds.

Rig Veda 10.9, as quoted in Ralph T H Griffith,
The Hymns of the Rigveda (1896)

The Hindu god Shiva is also particularly associated with this cycle of destruction and regeneration. In one story, his aggressive dance is so wild and out of control that the Earth is nearly destroyed, but afterwards the Earth is made fertile again. Shiva is not just the god of destruction, he is the god of resurrection too. It is not too much of a leap to see the seal showing the rape of Mother Nature as a precursor to later Shivaite philosophy and imagery; the key Shivaite symbols of the bull and the phallus are present and violence is shown to be a critical step towards regeneration.

Another seal appears even closer to the representation of Shiva that is familiar today. Seal number 420 as the archaeological record has it, or the *Proto-Shiva Seal*, shows a male figure sitting cross-legged in a yogic position. The eyes are crossed as if in deep meditation. On his head he wears a headdress of buffalo horns and his penis is on display. The buffalo horns and the phallus are symbols closely related to Shiva today; indeed Shiva is often represented and worshipped as a stylised stone phallus known as a Shiva lingam. The first written record of Shiva occurs in the *Rig Veda*, where several references are made to him using his earlier name of Rudra. However, the archaeological evidence presented by this ancient city suggests that the concepts of Shiva went back much further and that the Shiva described in the *Rig Veda* has his origins in pre-Hindu religions of the Indus plains.

Mohenjo Daro was abandoned around 1700BCE. At first it was thought that this was a result of the eastward sweep of Aryan invaders, and the marks of violent wounds on skeletons found in some of the last-inhabited houses seemed to back this up. However, more recent excavation has discredited this view and it now seems that the abandonment of Mohenjo Daro was not violent and sudden but rather came at the end of a steady decline in the fortunes of the city and the civilisation as a whole. Indeed, ironically, it seems that the decline was caused by the Indus River, the very thing that had given it such abundant life and prosperity in the preceding centuries.

The river's effects were gradual. Excavations show that in the early second millennium BCE, parts of the Mohenjo Daro mound became waterlogged as a result of increasingly frequent flooding. The ground floors of some houses became uninhabitable and were filled with rubble to allow the building of extensions on top. The numerous wells were extended above the water level to prevent them being polluted, and today in the areas where excavation has cleared down to the earlier (lower) buildings, the wells stick up above the ground. The decline in the civilisation is marked by the deteriorating quality of bricks of the upper parts of these well walls in comparison to the lower earlier sections. Mohenjo Daro's best days were behind it. Around the same time, the ceremonial bath fell into disuse and was filled with rubble. The river and its water had turned against the city and perhaps in retaliation, or perhaps out of exhaustion, the people of Mohenjo Daro turned their back on their water ceremonies.

One theory is that the river became destructive because of glacial blockages in the mountainous higher reaches. This would have meant several years of lighter flow, reducing trading and agriculture, followed by catastrophic flooding as the dam burst and the river released its stored volume.

So if Shiva was invented here, why didn't he die with the civilisation? Why weren't the beliefs of the proto-Shiva buried in the rubble of the ceremonial bath? We can only guess at the answer but to me the most convincing theory is that the character of the Shiva of Mohenjo Daro was already a powerful and sometimes violent one. The eventual destruction of the civilisation by natural forces associated with Shiva therefore strengthened rather than weakened the god's reputation. The three gods of the Hindu trinity are Brahma the creator, Vishnu the preserver and Shiva the destroyer. We can only guess, but it seems likely that Shiva's position in the all-powerful *trimurti* and his reputation as the destroyer of the universe had its foundations in what happened to Mohenjo Daro.

I sat outside the dak-bungalow on my last evening. I wrote with dust-covered fingers, listening to the insects' electric noises:

Shiva lives on the mountain at the source but he was born on the plains. He destroyed the city that had created him. If this city was his eggshell he broke it as he hatched. Now his birthplace is dusty, dry and empty. The name it was given is Mohenjo Daro, the City of the Dead. The river has moved again in the centuries since Mohenjo Daro was abandoned, it shifts often in these flat plains where there are no hills to direct its course. Now it flows a mile to the east and you cannot even see it from the highest point in the city.

A few miles upriver is the island of Sadhubela, lying in the Indus between the twin towns of Sukkur and Rohri. In this part of the desert the river runs through hard limestone and it is a protruding block of this limestone that forms this tiny island. Extraordinarily, it remains a holy Hindu site, right in the middle of Pakistan. I needed to get a special permit to visit, as it is seen as a potential target for Muslim extremists. The fisherman I asked to take me across studied my pass carefully; he would be in trouble, he said, if I had forged it. I promised him it was genuine.

I could see the *chowkidar* (keeper) of the temples waiting on the landing ghat as I approached. He had appeared almost as soon as we pushed the boat off and now he stood still, watching me drift towards him as we rowed in, hands behind his back and shoulders drooping like a wilted sentry. I could see his grey hair and his grey shalwar kameez, and hanging from one hand a wide ring of keys, gaoler style. I didn't know if I should wave or call a greeting – we had both been watching each other for so long it seemed a strange thing to suddenly say hallo. Above him a leafless tree was full of crows and they watched too, with beaks open wide. I expected to hear them cawing but as we got closer I realised that like all the other animals they too had been silenced by the sun.

'Sadhubela,' the chowkidar said to me as I climbed the ghat steps.

'Namaste,' I replied.

'Namaste, namaste...' He nodded as if agreeing that namaste was the word he had meant to start with.

He rattled his keys and I followed him to the temples, which were situated around a concrete courtyard. The largest was dedicated to Swami Bankhandi, the Hindu ascetic who first established a community on the island in the nineteenth century. Inside, a dark hall gave on to a low-roofed cell where a pale marble statue of the ascetic sat cross-legged, with striking black eyes staring straight ahead. Offerings of white sweets (the same I had seen at the Muslim

Sufi shrines) and small rupee notes were crumpled around his knees and curling trails of incense thickened the air.

There was another visitor sitting silently in front of the statue. He didn't turn to look at me but continued staring at the two black eyes, motionless and unblinking. He began praying and I could still hear him out in the courtyard. His prayers sounded conversational, with the intonation of questions and natural pauses for thought. He chanted his questions then replied to himself in a falsetto, pleading, sobbing and laughing like a little child. His two voices sounded so different that for a moment I wondered whether I had missed the child who was in there with him, crying and cooing and pleading. There was a sadness in this one man speaking to himself and his two-voiced-prayers seemed to mourn the loneliness of this island isolated by water and by religion. They seemed to describe the existence of the single Hindu chowkidar on this drop of Hindu land with little company except for the occasional visitor and a tree full of open-beaked crows.

The Shiva temple was a waist-high cell beneath a huge pointed spire of a roof. A tree grew from the back of the cell, through the concrete, stretching its shading branches over the courtyard. Inside was a circular dish full of white wax and sprinkled with petals and behind it the shiny black stone lingam – the phallus that represents Shiva in so many temples. A little further on was a two-storey building with another Shivaite altar on the roof where a lingam pointed towards a suspended brass bowl of water, bearing the salutation *om*. Then at the upriver point of the island a final lingam perched on a crumbling red brick altar. Beyond this stretched a bed of marshy reeds, half river, half island, before the open water continued milky and hazy up to the regular blocks of the Sukkur barrage to the north.

I sat in the shaded living quarters with the chowkidar and drank tea.

'I am from Sukkur.' He told me. 'My father and my grandfather were born here. They were knife makers.'

'Why did you not leave to India when the Hindus left?' That was the thing I always wondered about Hindus living in Pakistan. Before Partition they had been around 15 to 20 per cent of the population; now they were only 1 per cent. What was special about the ones who had stayed behind?

'My father did not want to. He had his business here. There was no reason to leave.' I wondered why his father felt it was safe enough to stay when Hindu businesses were being destroyed all over Pakistan. Was there some special position that his father had, some special relationship with his Muslim neighbours? But all he would say was yes, we had Muslim friends. He had never been to India. The furthest he had been was Islamabad.

He showed me his identity card, a youthful black-and-white photograph and the acronym MAD for the Minority Affairs Department, his government employers.

'You must get lonely here.'

'People visit. At the festival for three days many people visit. Hundreds.'

'Where do they come from?'

'From the country, from Karachi, from all over Pakistan.'

'From India?'

'No, not possible. Only Pakistani Hindus.'

I couldn't even imagine this island with crowds of people; it seemed such a quiet, forgotten place. 'When is the festival?'

'In ten days' time.' This was a surprise. I had intended to spend a day on the island then move on upriver but now I knew about the festival I was keen to see it. My plans were rapidly readjusted. Back on shore that afternoon I visited the office of the Evacuee Trust Property Board and organised a three-day permission slip to cover the festival. Then I went and waited for ten days away from the river, in the blissful cool of the hill stations to the west in Balochistan.

The cool of the highlands made the return to Sukkur even more painful. The temperature touched 50°C during the day and even the night air was cloying. The concrete walls and floor acted like storage heaters, radiating the daytime heat back at me all night and my hotel fan barely stirred it. I found a pharmacy that sold frozen bottles of water and clasped them to me to help me sleep, and when thirst and heat combined to wake me from feverish dreams I had cool water. I have never drunk so much water in my life, seven litres per day, and it all came out in sweat in my shalwar kameez, leaving it stiff and swirled with powdery salt tidemarks.

On my first visit, the river shore at Sukkur had looked drab and melancholy. The sand was dark and held scum-rimmed pools of forgotten river. Fishing nets were hung between poles to dry and stray dogs slept in their patchy shade. The predominant colour was grey.

Now it was festival day and the shore dazzled with a chaotic sea of veils and hats. The women's *dupattas* sparkled with mirrored fringes which matched the reflective bindis between their eyes and the curling arabesques of sequins running from their brows round to their cheekbones. Fine strings of gold ran between their nose studs and their earrings. Their wide, black eyes were lined with kohl and extended at the side into upturned almond shapes, but they quickly turned away from strange men. It looked like every one of the women was on the way to her own wedding.

The festival crowds stretched from the road all the way along to a sandbank where Mohana fishermen lined up their boats to ferry passengers across. Today the boats were decked with bunting and red and white pennants flew from bow and stern. They gracefully crossed the stream, laden with the silk-wrapped crowds and looking like elaborate floating flower arrangements. The Hindu families threw offerings – halves of banana, bags of petals and rupee notes – into the holy river. Crowds of Mohana children swam or waded on the sandbanks and claimed the prizes, glistening and spurting fountains of water from their mouths like spirits of the river.

On the ghat, huge food preparations were underway. Tin baths of chickpeas and shiny steel buckets of vegetables waited beside fire pits. Carton after carton of ghee was poured into circular pots big enough to boil a man in. People along the path gave out iced water and sherbet in metal cups chained to their stalls. '*Pani, pina, sherbet, pina*' they called, 'drink water, drink sherbet'. Above their basins were pictures of the gods they were serving: a flute-playing Krishna, a quizzical Ganesh, a benign Shiva.

The crowds of pilgrims flowed up the ghats and around the little temples. All the doors had been opened and the idols were polished with oil and decked with fresh marigold necklaces. They looked down with satisfied smiles, watching the piles of offerings accumulate. Elsewhere in Pakistan, the Hindu temples I had seen were dirty and crumbling as though they had not been cared for since the Hindus left over fifty years ago. It was strange to see Hindu temples that were so alive.

I remembered the temple stuck behind the cafés on Karachi's Gadani beach that I had seen a month before. A plaque outside announced that it had been completed in 1940 by a local family. After Partition it was abandoned, which meant it had only been in use for seven years. The tiles on the outside had begun to crumble, probably helped on their way by dogmatic believers who had chipped off anything that might suggest idolatry. A scene showed Hindu gods riding on great curling waves but their faces had been scratched away revealing the blank plaster underneath. Inside, betel juice stained the walls and the air smelled of old urine. Birds nested in the shelter of the arches and what might have been an entrance hall was now a mess of crumbled concrete and twisted reinforcement poles. A dead kitten lay among the rubble.

On my way through Pakistan I would come across more of these obsolete temples. In Rawalpindi, the elongated diamond of the *gopuram*, the characteristically Hindu ornate gateway, stuck up from the skyline in front of my hotel. When I went to the door to see inside it was opened by a policeman who showed me the peeling frescoes and stained tile work. It was now being used as a barrack house and was full of charpoys and officers taking their afternoon siestas. In Dera Ismail Khan I stayed in a temple that had been converted into a hotel. Although a lot of these buildings were not old, they were part of some era that had now passed. This made Sadhubela feel so much stranger; Hinduism and its buildings were unexpectedly alive here.

I met Victor John on the roof of the Shiva temple.

'The boatman told me that a foreigner had come. I have been looking for you. My name is Victor John. I am a Christian pastor.'

'A Christian?' He looked like other Hindu visitors: dark Sindhi complexion, moustache, shalwar kameez.

'I come here every year with my Christian friends. We are Christian converts. We make friendships with the Hindu people and then we visit them later in their houses and try to make them come to Jesus. Please let me show you around.'

My heart sank. I had come here to see how the tiny minority of Hindus celebrated in Pakistan, and now I was stuck walking around with an evangelical Christian on a proselytising mission. Weren't the Hindus a threatened enough minority here, without the additional pressure of Christian missionaries? I felt defensive.

'Why do you try to convert the Hindus? Why try to convert anyone? Why not the Muslim people? There are more of them.'

He looked at me disbelievingly. 'That would not be allowed. The government would not allow us to do that. We can only preach to Hindus.'

As he told me about his work, though, slowly my view of him changed.

At each shrine he stood with me, but his friends, who he said had converted to Christianity, knelt before the idols and clasped their hands. Despite their Christian names and prayers it seemed there was still a lot of the old belief alive in them. One told me about his wedding the previous year. It had taken place in a church but the celebration and some of the ritual had been unmistakably Hindu. It had lasted for two days and at the end they had walked around the Hindu sacred fire inside the church. He said it was important in his predominantly Hindu community that these symbols were present because they were so closely connected with marriage.

'If we did not walk around the fire then people would not believe we really are married.' Victor John's friends described themselves as 'Hindu-Christians', which I think was partly to distance themselves from the pariah and illegal status of Islamic converts to Christianity, and partly to explain their cultural background.

Victor John explained how most of the people at the festival, indeed many of the Hindus in Pakistan, came from the Cholistani tribes of eastern Sindh and The Punjab. They were semi-nomadic people, self-sufficient and desert dwelling. On Partition they were not threatened in the same way as Hindus in the rest of Pakistan and may not even have been aware of the political developments that put their tracts of desert together with Pakistan rather than India. They never saw any reason to migrate and now they made up a large part of the Hindu Pakistani minority, minding their own business out in the empty deserts that border Rajasthan in India.

Now, as these tribespeople retreat from their nomadism they are encountering difficulties in the state schools. Part of Victor John's work was to set up independent schools for them. 'First, education is important. Then after, if they want to come to Jesus then they will. If they do not want to, it is up to them. It is for them to decide. We do not force any conversion because what is the point of that.'

Victor John pointed out the traditional dress of the Cholistani tribeswomen. 'It is Christmas for them!' Their arms were fully encased in stacks of bangles.

Among the throng of tribespeople were a few slick-looking metropolitan Hindus from the tiny communities that remain in Karachi and Lahore. These younger men wore tight jeans, Bollywood T-shirts and big buckled loafers. They laid damp facecloths over perfectly gelled hair and wandered around languidly toying with dark glasses and eyeing up the sheepish girls in their kilograms of tribal jewellery.

There was an arch between the Shiva temple and another part of the complex which caught the river breeze and we sat there for the midday hour. Later in the day, as it cooled, we visited the concrete bath where pilgrims took ritual showers beneath piped Indus water and wandered among the tented trinket stalls. There were Vishnu key rings, Hanuman key rings, glass bangles and incense, and for twenty rupees a man with a battery-powered tattoo needle would inscribe your name in blue ink on your wrist.

The chowkidar spent the whole of the festival in the library. This was partly because there was no clear filing system and his knowledge was required in order to find books for the more scholarly visitors, but also I suspect because the chowkidar didn't really like crowds of people. For 363 days a year this island was a solitary place and he was used to that. During the festival the library was the only vaguely quiet place left.

He greeted me with a weary smile and led me to the book he had promised to look out for me ten days before, the English translation of *Life of Sri Swami Bankhandi Sahib,* the founder of Sadhubela as a Hindu island. It was a classic hagiography, similar to those of Christian and Buddhist saints; collections of stories to inspire and fascinate.

The Indus played a central role in this saint's life and work. Having travelled through Assam, Brahmapur, Madras, Malabar, Thatta, Karachi and Hyderabad, it was on this island that he decided to stay. As detailed in the book he explained,

… the Hindu scriptures have praised the sacred river Indus… Before the Mahomedan rule a big Kumbh Fair was held there; I desire to pass the remaining days of my life on the bank of such a river.

The river features in the miracles that he performed. He calmed its currents to save a drowning milkman; he had the currents transport a gold bangle back to the island's ghats; he prevented a boat from capsizing and, in the case of an already capsized boat, he had its wreck land on the island so that the sadhu ascetics that lived with him could use it for a shelter. He retrieved a drowned boy from the current and transported him to his mother's garden, drying his clothes in the process; he successfully ordered the river not to rise above a certain point on his island and, at one point (for no clear reason), he turned the Indus water into ghee.

He was said to be good friends with Jhulelal, the Hindu water deity, and the pair of them would promenade on the surface of the Indus, Jhulelal on his smiling pala fish and Swami Bankhandi in a pair of wooden sandals that raised him several inches above the water.

Snakes also feature heavily in the life of the saint. This is not surprising, as Hinduism often associates snakes with water. Before Swami Bankhandi had built any temples or shelters it was the snakes of the island who formed a shade for him to sleep under. It was one of these snakes that asked Swami Bankhandi to stay on the island and advised him to plant banyan trees there. Swami Bankhandi's relations with snakes were similar to Shiva's; Shiva is often shown wearing a snake as a scarf, and the book tells us:

… sometimes they wreathed themselves around Sri Swami's neck, sometimes they entwined round the arm making arm bangles. Some times they encircled round his upper arm as an armlet for it and sometimes they wove round his ankles as anklets and sometimes they served as earrings.

In order to protect the island, Swami Bankhandi miraculously produced 56 warriors and six heroes and made them live in disguise to prevent against the interference of 'ghosts, giants and witches'.

However, protection was also required from the interference of the British who visited the island in 1862, intending to use it to support one of the legs of a planned railway bridge. Immediately on landing at the ghat the Sukkur collector (governor), a certain Mr Campbell, and the railway engineer were both struck down by chronic stomach pains. Swami Bankhandi provided the men with holy ashes as a cure and in return they agreed not to build the bridge using his land. The Lansdowne Bridge, as it was named, still stands across the river using a different island to support the central span. The river is slightly wider at this point, but although it is a less obvious crossing point, it made sense to build it here and not annoy the powerful yogi.

On his death Swami Bankhandi asked for his grave to be the Indus. But the river would not accept him at first and his undecomposed body re-emerged from the depths some days later, untouched by the fish. For a second time his body was consigned to the water, this time with ceremony, grandeur, flowers and perfumes, and the Indus accepted the corpse.

I returned by boat to Sukkur to buy water and paan for the evening. At first I had been revolted by chewing paan; the red tongue and teeth looked pretty unattractive. But now I found its fresh mouthwash taste and mild stimulant effect made it perfect when the heat was oppressive. On my return the policeman got uncomfortable about letting me back on the island.

'You are what country? You are what purpose? You are Mussalman? Why you come here? You are Muslim?' The police have to prevent any Muslim from coming to the island during the festival in case they cause trouble, and with my paler skin and my height, I didn't look like the Sindhi Hindus.

I told him I was British and had a permission chit, and produced the headed notepaper. The policeman waved me through but I noticed that another followed me over to the island and watched me for a few hours until he got bored.

As the sun sank the pilgrims moved out on to the grass at the centre of the island. They crowded together on their mats and blankets like sunbathers on a Mediterranean beach, but instead of the sun they were bathing in the cool soft air that blew across the river.

A stage was set up at one end and a surreal and chaotic series of acts appeared. Hindi music blared out from scratchy speakers while boys were invited to come up and demonstrate their dancing. Then an overweight couple mimed and danced to Bollywood hits. They were followed by a priest who made a speech telling the men to leave alcohol, cigarettes and heroin and the women to forsake face powder, lipstick and all other make-up. A man came on stage with a ventriloquist's dummy but inexplicably left without performing. The dancers took over instead. I sat and chewed paan and enjoyed the darkness.

At 11 o'clock I retreated to the balcony of the ashram where Victor John had saved me a sleeping space. We ate rice served in the pages of a recycled Italian telephone directory, and then we watched the full moon, elongated in the ripples of the Indus. A wind blew in from the east and I felt tired. I covered my face with my shawl against mosquitoes and slept.

Before dawn, Victor John woke me to tell me he was leaving – he had a long journey back to Cholistan. Some time later a man lay down using the other side of my bag as a pillow.

In the yellow dawn I wandered the field in front of the stage. The grass was flattened and worn from the crowds, and scraps of rice-encrusted paper attracted meandering lines of ants. There were a few sleeping figures but most of the field was clear now. I could see the boats taking pilgrims back already – tired, quiet passengers who had no offerings left for the river.

At the Brahma ghat men were washing, stirring up plumes of foam from soap in their hair. Others sat on the steps rubbing their teeth thoughtfully with sticks or hawking and spitting phlegm into the water. On the mud banks by the ghat the river had deposited the offerings of petals from the day before, grimy now and mixed with juice cartons and other rubbish. Mohana kids were already up swimming alongside the ferry boats and running along the just submerged banks of silt so they looked like miniature Swami Bankhandis. They did not shout so loud now – they sensed this year's party was over.

I walked up to the tip of the island and sat by the brick altar and its chalky red phallus. The reed beds made an arrowhead, cutting the river and pointing to the hills of the north. I felt a growing affection for this great river that fed the country and its varied religious faiths. When I had first planned my journey the river had been a convenient route through a country that fascinated me, but now I saw that this understated its importance. The river is much more deeply part of the cities and shrines and the personality of this country. It is worshipped and it is used as a sewer. It created a civilisation and destroyed it. Without the Indus there would be no Pakistan, but the Indus enters the country from the arch-enemy, India.

The sun changed gear and flushed the day with heat and, already sweating, I walked back to the ghats. The boats going back to shore were nearly empty. The ashes in the cooking hearths were white and tents lay flat on the ground, ready for folding. I saw the chowkidar sweeping the library steps. He stood straight and raised a single hand in farewell.

Back in the Sukkur hotel I felt stale. My teeth were grainy with plaque. I had run out of water the previous evening and had drunk numerous bottles of Pepsi and Mirinda orange that had left my saliva custard-like and my teeth aching. On the shore I scrubbed away with a new toothbrush and took a long shower. Then I drank two bottles of water and ate some dates.

I spent the evening on my balcony looking out on to the clock tower in the main square of Sukkur. During the day the shops were quiet and the rubbish heaps around the clock tower stank in the sun. But with darkness the rubbish men came and cleared the pavements and the chai shops set out their ranks of tables like a huge outdoor café. A boy beat a car tyre inner tube full of ice to make the slush for sherbet. A steaming pan of oil bubbled as pakoras and wide, creased poppadoms fried. The mango sellers extended in a semicircle, their fruit graded in size and colour, sweet yellow Alphonsos and huge voluptuous Keitts in blushing green, all beneath a bare light bulb.

Looking directly down through the tangle of electrical wires I can see the bald spot on the paan seller's head where he sits cross-legged amid dishes of betel, molasses, coconut, different battered tins of dry flaky tobacco and the heart-shaped betel leaves already slathered with red paste – ready to wrap up the fragrant, bitter mouthfuls. The traffic still buzzes around the clock tower but the sound is muted in the darkness and the horns are outnumbered by the tinkling of bicycle bells. Donkeys attached to carts wait in rows around the clock railings, their ears doing the splits while they chew. The men who ride the carts sit to eat on the ranks of plastic tables.

People do not sit out and relax like this during the day but now it is night and the city can live again.

CHAPTER 5

KALABAGH AND MITHANKOT

To Dera Ismail Khan, the water of the Indus is of a lead colour; below that town it becomes of a dirty whitish yellow, tinged with red. In the freshes the red tint is heightened; but the general colour continues the same. Between Attock and Mittun all the streamlets that fall into the Indus are of a bright red; save the Hurroo and Toe, which have pebbly beds and clean water.

Lieutenant John Wood, *Report on the River Indus*, in Appendix II of *Cabool*, Sir Alexander Burnes (John Murray, 1842)

At dawn the day after the Sadhubela festival I caught the Khyber Mail train from Sukkur to Khanpur, hoping to cross the river to the west bank by the road bridge marked on my map. After the heat of the night and the early start I felt drugged. I dozed in my seat, my head lolling and banging against the bars on the window, waking me up painfully, fuzzy eyed and greasy faced.

With the dawn came dust-strained light and the first movements of waking villages. Graveyards introduced us to them, wilted black and green flags sprouting from the hard packed earth around the headstones. Charpoys had been set out in the open air of the fields at night so that families could sleep in the breeze and now they were being pulled into the shade for the day, leaving sledge tracks in the dust. Scenes appeared for a moment as we trundled past. A troop of water buffalo trudging wearily towards the milk house, oblivious to the shouts and flying stones of the cowherd. *They will get there in their own time.* Three camels, a family group, large, medium and small, plucking at a single thorn bush with insensitive pouting lips. Dabs of colour on a grey canvas as a procession of women shuffle along a raised embankment carrying water pots on their heads. Fields flooded from irrigation channels, the water standing in furrows and reflecting the sky so that the ground is striped pale blue and chocolate brown like the tie of an exclusive gentlemen's club.

I stood in the breeze of the open carriage door watching the edges of rail-side settlements and felt like I was seeing the trailers to a film, a momentary introduction to a story that I would never see more of … and we moved steadily on.

At each station there was an arrival time and a departure time and enough time in between for tea and a slice of dry breakfast cake. The railway stations were orderly and clean. Each one had a polished brass departure bell and a clock tower. The attendants were in uniform, the guards in buff, the officious ticket clerks blue and the porters in wide red turbans to help them carry heavy cases on their heads. The trains had their own Pakistan Railways livery, which made them look like antique packing cases – dark green at the top and bottom with a red and white stripe in the centre, the white faded to an old-patina beige, many times repainted and rubbed with dust and bodies so it looked like polished leather.

There was still something in these carriages that spoke of the ambitious British colonial projects that first laid tracks across the desert.

But the first big British transit project in this area was concerned not with railways but with river transport. It was up the Indus River that the British Empire first extended an inquisitive tentacle into Sindh in 1830. Alexander Burnes, the famous Great Game explorer and diplomat, was in charge of the mission. Under the pretext of sending a present of two dray horses to Maharaja Ranjit Singh, Burnes was to sail a boat from the coast up the Indus and then up the Ravi tributary, finally crossing by land to the Maharaja's palace in Lahore.

The huge horses were extremely well received. They were so much bigger than the native horses that the Maharaja's stable decked them out with elephant howdahs rather than saddles. However, the real reason for this expedition was not to deliver a couple of horses but rather to survey the navigability of the Indus as a route to the absorption of another province into the British Raj. It was a sly plan and there was opposition from within the British government. Sir Charles Metcalfe, the Governor-General of India, wrote at the time that it was:

… a trick… unworthy of our Government… just such a trick as we are often falsely suspected and accused of by the native powers of India, and this confirmation of their suspicions… will do us more injury… than any advantage to be gained…

James Lunt *Bokhara Burnes* (Faber & Faber, 1969)

Swami Bankhandi, the Hindu holy man who settled on Sadhubela, had already foreseen British conquest even before Burnes's ship sailed past his island, and had warned a group of Muslims who had victimised him that they would soon lose power to white men. Fourteen years later General Sir Charles Napier would annex Sindh on a weak pretext and famously cable the news that another kingdom had been added to the British Empire with the pithy one-word telegram: 'Peccavi.' I have sinned.

But there was one more investigative voyage up the Indus nine years before Napier invaded. Burnes was involved in this second trip too, but this time so was a young naval officer, Lieutenant John Wood. The instructions he was given by Burnes made the purpose of the mission quite clear:

You are aware that one of the objects of this expedition is to ascend the Indus from its mouth to Attock, that a more perfect knowledge of the river may be procured, as well for the purposes of commerce as of war...

Captain John Wood *A Journey to the Source of the River Oxus*
(second edition, John Murray, 1872)

Both men would later write memoirs about their journeys up the Indus and despite both being Scottish military men from similar backgrounds what emerges from these accounts is a picture of two very different characters. Burnes comes across as a swashbuckling, imperial playboy, part of a generation of confident players in the imperial game. He was born in Montrose, the son of the local provost who was first cousin of the poet Robert Burns, and he seems to have shared Robert's weakness for women. At Shikarpur, a town in the lower reaches of the river, he was fascinated by a festival involving girls in wet saris.

According to Burnes's memoir *Cabool* (1842), they 'prostrated themselves in the canal and prayed... Shikarpoor can certainly boast of the bright eyes of its daughters; and this day gave us an excellent opportunity of judging of them.' On his first trip up the Indus he fondly remembered in Lahore watching a display of a battle between drunk dancing girls who were handsomely rewarded for tearing and scratching each other. Burnes was later to say that he looked back on those two weeks in Lahore as the happiest in his life. This weakness for women was to catch up with him and was a contributing factor in his murder in Kabul at the hands of local men just ten years later.

Beyond the women of Sindh, Burnes took a romantic joy in the other exotic pleasures of travel. He enjoyed smoking hashish in the evening, a pleasure he had been introduced to on his first visit to India aged sixteen. He wrote enthusiastically about adding to his list of culinary experiences by eating crocodile steak and in Lahore he enjoyed heavy drinking sessions with the decadent, chronically ugly, amir. According to James Lunt's *Bokhara Burnes* (1969), Burnes summed up the usefulness of the Indus and at the same time gave an insight into his lifestyle when he described how the river route reduced the cost of imported luxuries to West Punjab:

As the good river Indus is a channel for luxuries as well as commerce, I can place before my friends at one-third in excess of the Bombay price my champagne, hock, madeira, sherry, port, claret, sauterne… hermetically sealed salmon…

Lieutenant John Wood was born in Perth, not far from Burnes's Montrose, but his outlook and character were in stark contrast. From the very mouth of the Indus he was unimpressed, describing the marsh and mangrove swamps in his book, *A Journey to the Source of the River Oxus*, as having a 'dreary and unpromising aspect'. He rarely found anything to enthuse about, and when he did he used dry, scientific terms of praise. Wood was an expert on steam navigation and his concerns were always with the business and logistical aspects of the journey. After his Indus trip he would travel to other parts of the expanding British Empire as part of the New Zealand Company then later to the colony of Victoria in Australia. After these postings, his knowledge of river-borne transit enabled him to return to India as head of the Oriental Inland Steam Navigation Company and subsequently as manager of the Indus Steam Flotilla.

The division of labour was clear. Wood was to concentrate on navigation and fuel supply while Burnes was the diplomat and the charmer. In Wood's account the types of forest on the riverbank, wind direction and even the changing colour of the tributaries were all meticulously noted. In Burnes's account the detail is in the conversation with local dignitaries.

I often wondered what it would have been like to travel with them on my trip. It would never have been boring with Burnes and no doubt his highly developed affability would have helped in dealing with officials when buildings were closed or visas expired. But with Burnes there was always the risk of adventure. The tricky situations that he was so good at talking himself out of would inevitably be his fault to begin with. Wood would have been less interesting but far more reliable. Visas would not expire in the first place. Trains would never be missed.

There is no clue in either of their accounts as to how they got on together during their journey up to Attock. Nineteenth-century travel writing didn't speak of such things. I imagine Burnes reveling in seeing uncharted territory, talking with the boat men across the hashish pipe in the evening. I imagine him already dressed in the loose-fitting native clothes that he would fully adopt by the time he was in Kabul, and that he wore to have his portrait painted some years later. I imagine Wood still in his naval officer's uniform, constantly note taking, still pale under his sun helmet. The only insight we have into what Burnes thought of Wood comes in his report to the Governor-General of India, quoted in the preface to the second edition of *A Journey to the Source of the River Oxus* (1872):

The unremitting attention of this officer throughout will be apparent to his Lordship in Council in the perusal of his clear and practical report, while his own zeal and assiduity appear in the precision, variety, and extent of the information.

The praise is sincere and with a reputation like that Wood would go far, but I can't help thinking that between the lines there is a hint that Burnes found him a little boring.

Their deaths reflected their lives. Burnes died aged 36, murdered in Kabul. He had been warned that his life was in danger and he should move to the well-guarded British cantonment two miles outside the city, but he ignored the advice. He had a reputation for having affairs and treating Afghan women as harlots which was extremely dangerous given the Pashtun code of honour. In the cantonment he was described as lacking moral self-restraint. But despite this dangerous reputation he chose to stay, perhaps to continue his romantic but ill-advised liaisons. Even when a mob gathered in the city and rumours circulated that his life was in danger, Burnes refused to withdraw to the fortified cantonment. On the evening of 2 November 1841 his apartment was burned and he was killed along with his brother.

Wood died aged 59, thirty years after Burnes. His son, in the introduction to his father's account of the voyage up the Indus, wrote that the illness that killed him was a result of a hurried journey to Simla in the height of the hot season, undertaken in the interest of his employers, the Indus Steam Flotilla. Just as Burnes's wild ways ended up killing him, so it seems that Wood's sense of duty and fastidiousness brought about his death. Wood's flotilla was to have a limited life because the flatness of Sindh, which made for a slow, silted, difficult-to-navigate river, made the land next to it perfect for laying down rails. By 1860, just 24 years after Burnes's and Wood's voyage, railway lines would take the place of rivers as the main conduit for trade.

Wood's fleet had long since rotted but there were other relics of the Empire still on the river where they had been used to cross the water. I had been told there were old English boats at Mithankot on the other side of the river. However, the bridge marked on my map was a misprint: at Khanpur there was nothing but a huge expanse of flat water stretching to a woolly green horizon. Instead, small boats shuttled passengers back and forth, gliding steadily across, pointing diagonally upstream. We passed one on its way back, full of people and with a Suzuki van as wide as the boat precariously balanced on two planks, looking ready to topple in at any moment. The driver was sitting in the van waving at us and hooting his horn.

'Where is the old English boat?' I asked in the hotel at Mithankot.

'Down at the river.' But around here the river was mercurial and pulled away from its course into marsh-clogged irrigation channels and old backwaters where it once ran strong. 'Go on the track to the small bridge.'

The sad hulk of the old boat was, indeed, moored downriver of a small bridge leaning slightly to one side so that the funnel pointed upwards at a drunken angle. The paintwork was peeling but I could still see the red stripe around the bow and the lettering *Indus Que-n*. The second e was gone. The man who took the tolls on one of the side-channel bridges showed me how to climb up on to the captain's bridge so that I could look down on the deck, shaded from the sun by a rust-scabbed corrugated tin roof. On the bridge was the pulley device, still in good condition and branded Fishers Ltd. Engineers. Paisley. At the bow was another one: T. Reid & Sons. Engineers. Paisley.

'When did she go across?' I asked the bridge man.

'When I was young she was crossing the river many times a day. Across all the way to Khanpur with a thousand passengers and trucks too. But now she cannot cross. There are new islands now.' Today the river is significantly lower and the edges are a maze of shallow channels and islands. The large *Indus Queen* has too deep a draught to navigate these so she is permanently confined to this clogged channel to gradually list and rot. Vehicles must now take their chances balanced on smaller boats or drive the long way round via the bridge at Dera Ghazi Khan.

The *Indus Queen* is now used as a hotel for those who reach the river too late to cross and by the builders who come to repair the bridges and causeways of the side channels. Charpoys were spread out on the deck in the shade of the corrugated iron roof. In return for the questions that I had asked him about the ferries the bridge man asked me about my country.

'What is your currency? What animals do you have? What fruit do you have? How many buffalo does your father own?'

'None.'

'None? How much is a buffalo?'

'I'm not sure. I've never bought a whole one. Only pieces of a cow.'

'How much is a piece of a cow? How much is a mango?'

I wondered how much the shrink-wrapped mangoes cost in the supermarket. 'Maybe 100 rupees?'

'Wah. It is a rich man than eats mangoes in Scotland.'

'And they are not very nice because they come by aeroplane from faraway places, so they are not as sweet as the mangoes here.'

'Wah, Wah. A rich man and a stupid one.'

He was half joking – acting out his surprise – purposefully playing the part of the innocent rural Pakistani who has never seen the world. He was trying to make me feel welcome and entertained.

Further up the banks he showed me another rusting hulk. This was a paddle steamer, but the paddles had rotted, leaving only their circular metal skeleton and making the boat look like an amphibious combine harvester. The machinery was all above deck, as the advantage of a paddle steamer is that it has a much shallower draught than a conventional propeller boat and can work on shallower water. This would have been able to cross for several years after the *Indus Queen* could not. I swung the boiler doors open, revealing the exhaust tubes that ran into twin funnels now partially blocked with birds' nests.

I felt the childish excitement that I used to feel on family holidays on farms, where the old tractors were left to decay in the fields and we would spend hours playing on them. The sandy patina of rusted metal, the melting valves and bronchial pipes and the smell of old oil and dust and iron.

This nameless paddle steamer was a newer vessel but its machinery still bore those imperial brands – 'McKenzie & Co Engineers. Karachi', 'Chadburns Ship Telegraph Co Ltd. Liverpool' – with its big brass handle and the telegraph orders running around the circular dial: Full Ahead, Half, Slow, Stop. Full Astern, Half, Slow. Stop.

The chain pulley still worked. Although it had not been oiled for years it still turned when I pulled it and began to reel in slowly – inch by inch. Up the chain came, link by rusty link, winding itself around the spindle of the wheel. Finally the last link came in, clinking across the deck and hanging loosely. It was not attached to anything anymore.

Another clinking came from the riverbank – a goatherd was trailing a flock of white goats, each with the upper part of its head dyed orange with henna. They followed him obediently.

There was a haze of cloud in the sky now and a breath of wind over the water. It was pleasantly cool. Birds circled over the reedy islands, flashing white patches on the underside of their wings like the glint of mirrors in the sun. A tractor purred in the dust thrown up by its wheels. The goats followed their goatherd into a field and an old man cycled along the raised embankment with three milk cans lashed to his carrier, going just fast enough not to topple over.

I remembered what another soldier of the Empire, eighty years later than Burnes, had written – a piece of writing that was so evocative of the evenings of the Indian subcontinent:

It was "cow-dust hour." Ox-carts creaked slowly to a mud-walled village… men and beasts were gentle and well content. An infinite serenity lay under all that sky.

F Yeats-Brown *Bengal Lancer* (1930).

A raven perched next to me on the ship's bridge, cawing, and I hissed at it to go away and leave me alone in the lovely peace of the riverbank. I was overcome with a tremendous sense of warmth and contentment. A feeling that in a world that always seems imperfect, my particular place in that moment could not have been bettered. As if all the various internal and external stimuli that make us feel were somehow pushing in the same direction. I was alone on a rusty ship with the heat of the day subsiding. Later I would go back to the hotel at Mithankot, there would be tea and chapatti, and then I would share the rest of my packet of Player's Gold Flake with the hotel owner and tomorrow I would move on upriver. There was nothing remarkable in any of this but that didn't matter. Sometimes the way our experiences affect us converge in a way that makes us feel simple contentment.

There was meant to be another British boat two hours upriver at Dera Ismail Khan. This was the SS *Jhelum*, which had begun life in the Royal Navy and had seen service in southern Iraq during World War I. But when I arrived at where it was meant to be tied up, the bank was empty. The *Jhelum* had sunk a few years earlier when the river was high. There was nothing to do but sit in a riverside *chaikhana* and eat lunch.

The water stretched away to a hazed horizon but it was not a lazy river here. The water eddied into whirlpools at the side and boiled with impatience. Floating islands of leaves sped by in the strong currents. Hawks and ravens swooped out from the trees around the restaurant to pluck dead things from the flow.

I sat in the shade of the restaurant all afternoon. The river changed from clouded green to the flecked yellow of antique glass.

More cafés opened in the evening and set out red plastic tables on the riverbank. Stalls serving kulfi, spiced ice cream, were set up with their own council of stools on the shaded parts of the road. There was a fairground nearby and I climbed into the cage of a dilapidated

Ferris wheel that creaked around rheumatically, driven by a tractor engine. From the swinging top I could see the indecisive river heading south and the braided strands of marshy side channels. In between the channels were villages of bamboo-roofed huts where boys played with plastic-bag kites.

Another hundred miles upriver and, like the *Indus Queen* machinery, the rusting bridge at Kalabagh was Scottish too. 'McClellan & Son Ltd. Lutha Works, Glasgow, 1928,' said the plaque on the girders. Thirteen spans of brown metal paved with rotting planks and tarmac. It was built as a combined road and rail bridge with a narrow-gauge track set into the wood, but the railway had now been abandoned and at either end the tracks were buckled by invading tree roots. Under the cars and motorbikes the planks rattled and jumped against their loose bolts.

I could see Kalabagh as I walked across the bridge. It nestled in the fold of a mountain, its box-like houses making chaotic steps up the slope until they met the cliffs and could go no further. I remembered the different ways in which Burnes and Wood described the town. In *Cabool*, Burnes commented on the 'romantic cliffs' while Wood, in *A Journey to the Source of the River Oxus*, true to form, labelled it 'the hottest place between Attock and the sea, and it would require little trouble to prove it the most unhealthy.'

The houses in Kalabagh were all squint. Their balconies sloped and their pillars slanted at first inquisitively and then drunkenly towards the river. It looked as if they had been built to look deliberately quaint, like Disneyland castles, for the materials themselves did not look old. But the reality was that Kalabagh houses fall down very quickly; the town is built on seams of rock salt which are gradually being dissolved by water beneath the buildings' foundations.

The mountain above was red rock but fringed with white lines of salt like the evaporated sweat marks on my shalwar kameez. Where the Indus squeezed between the hills it had clawed at them, washing away the rock salt and leaving the sides scarred and broken. But above and below the defile the river deposited banks of fetid mud that were empty of vegetation because of the salinity.

I was more inclined to agree with Wood's summing up of Kalabagh. I was feeling ill as I walked the streets – maybe because of the heat, or the squint houses, or because I had overdone my paan chewing to try and give me energy. I stopped at an ice cream shop to recover. The ice cream maker was moustachioed and plump. He reminded me of the typical Italian-Scottish ice cream maker.

'Sit down, sit down. You are tired.'

So I sat down and drank iced water while he made ice cream. He filled a metal bucket with sweetened and spiced milk and secured a mixing spoon through the lid. Then he put it in a slatted wooden tub and packed blocks of ice round it. He poured rock salt over the ice to make it give out its coldness and attached the spoon to a petrol motor so that it whirled round and broke up the crystals.

After two bowls of kulfi topped with sweet white vermicelli, I was sent off with one of his sons to see the salt mines in the hill above. Wood had recorded the mining of salt, sulphur and alum in this very place, which he described in *A Journey to the Source of the River Oxus* as keeping 'its inhabitants in an atmosphere as noxious as it is disagreeable.'

A cool wind blew out of the mine tunnels and we stooped as we walked in. A minute of walking along the cramped entrance took us into a wide cavern with a roof that was red and glassy. The floor was covered with imperfect blocks where the salt was seamed with sand

and rock and it glistened with the razors of salt crystals. Sometimes the roof was thin or cracked and a thin light shone in from a distant sun. Sulphur oozed in white scabs from the salt and made the air ripe and eggy.

'I think this tunnel is safe, or this one. This one is falling in, I can't remember...' Tunnels stretched off left and right from the cavern and the ice cream maker's son's confusion was making me nervous.

'It is nice. Thank you for taking me but we should go out now,' I told him and we emerged with creased eyes to the glare of the day.

There were bigger mines further east, where truckloads of rock salt were transported out on underground roads, but small-scale local mining was still going on in Kalabagh. Outside, old men sat among the rubble and chipped red salt blocks from the rock. It was this rock salt that the ice cream maker had used to melt the ice. And to make salty breakfast tea in Kalabagh they stirred it with a stick of red salt.

At Kalabagh train station I left my bag with an old man waiting at the platform. I didn't think about it until after I had asked him. Would I leave my bag with a stranger in any other country? I wondered if the honesty of the people I met in rural Pakistan had made me over-confident of my safety.

I climbed up the dry hill above the station to where there were the ruins of a series of Jain temples. Pottery shards fanned out from the crumbling ledges where the temples sat. Many of the temples had fallen into pits as this hill was suffering from the same salt-seam erosion as Kalabagh. The originally vertical shikhara or spires of the temples leaned to one side where their foundations had worn away and some had collapsed altogether. The ground opened up in craters and the mountain set up its own monuments – great red spires of rock poking from the yellow rubble of fallen temples. But the temple at the top was safe. I climbed the fine masonry steps to the trefoiled arches. From the top I could see the green curl of the Indus carving round Kalabagh and turning south.

I wondered if the British sailors on the Indus Steam Flotilla, or the engineers who brought the girders over from Glasgow to make the thirteen arches of the Kalabagh bridge, ever made the fifteen-minute climb up to the Jain temple and considered that one day their monuments would crumble like this too.

The old man was asleep on the pillow of my rucksack. I bought him a Pepsi on the train to thank him. The train rattled away from the hills of the Indus but soon it met more hills and we clattered through tunnels cut into the ribs of this folded land. The tunnels were deafening with the trisyllabic battery of the wheels reflected back from sheer walls.

My ticket was for Attock city, which some still call by its old colonial name, Campbellpore. At the time I did not know which colonial figure Campbellpore was named after but I remember hoping that he might have been some ancestor of mine, and I hoped that having his name linked to this Punjabi city might have brought him as close to this land as I felt.[3] Close, and fascinated, just as

---

3 Campbellpore was actually named after Colin Campbell, 1st Baron Clyde, another buccaneering figure of the Empire with a character, rather like Burnes, both heroic and morally flawed. Despite his active military service, Campbell lived to the age of 71 and was buried in Westminster Abbey. Since my journey a biography has been published, *Victoria's Scottish Lion: The Life of Colin Campbell, Lord Clyde*, written by Adrian Greenwood (The History Press, 2015).

Burnes felt for his 'good river Indus', rather than Wood, who finally summed up the Indus thus:

In conclusion, we may remark, that there is no known river in either hemisphere, discharging even half the quantity of water than the Indus does, which is not superior for navigable purposes to this far-famed stream. In this practical age the beauty of a river is measured by its utility...

Captain John Wood *A Journey to the Source of the River Oxus*
(second edition, John Murray, 1872)

PART II PAKISTAN

THE MOUNTAINS: SWAT AND THE KARAKORUM

CHAPTER 6

THE SWAT VALLEY

Swat, the homeland of many of the Pashtun tribes, is a strip of land lying between the Indus on the east and Afghanistan to the west, with Peshawar to the south and the Shandur range to the north. My Pakistani friends had always been keen to impress on me how safe their country was, but they warned me to be careful in two places, Karachi and Swat. Karachi, as the huge lawless and often violent metropolis where bad people go to hide, and Swat, as the patchily autonomous area neighbouring on the porous Afghan borderlands, were both areas where anti-West sentiment was more strongly felt and where the law had less control.

The first bus stop I waited at after entering the region consisted of a shed at the junction of the roads north to Chitral and east to Mingora. There was a single charpoy next to a tea stall and I sat next to a stocky man with a fist-length beard and skullcap.

'You are not from here?' He spoke in Urdu. Often people spoke to me in Pashtun because they took me for an Afghan or a Pashtun; with my scruffy over-the-shoulder bag, my pale skin, my bushy hair and my height I looked like one of the many Pashtuns who flock to the big cities to find work. It did me no harm to be considered a Pashtun, as they have a reputation for standing up for themselves. But he'd recognised I would not speak Pashtun.

I replied, 'I am from the north.'

He looked at me more closely. 'Chitrali?' Chitral was about fifty miles north of the Mingora bus stop.

'That is the direction of my home, but I am from still further north than Chitral.'

'You are Pakistani.' Then he examined me again. Although he was not old I noticed one of his eyes was clouded over and he turned his head so his good eye was looking at me directly. Realisation dawned on his face; his eyes lit up triumphantly. 'You are a Tajik.'

With the caution that had been drummed into me I knew it would have been safer for him not to know I was a Westerner but I hated to lie, even if I might have got away with it, and there was a kindness in his face that stopped me.

'No Sir. I am from a country many hundreds of miles from here, near to Inglistan. I am a traveller.'

'Wah. From Inglistan. You are very welcome.' He pumped my hand and turned his eye on me again, as if now remembering the looks of a Westerner. 'You must have seen many countries. Tell me, what countries you have seen?'

I told him a list of countries and to each one he sighed, 'Wah, wah.' Then I asked him. 'What countries have you seen, Ji?'

'I have seen Pakistan,' he paused for a second, remembering a journey, 'and Afghanistan, I have relatives who live there. And there is one other country I have seen but it is far away. Its name is Cuba.'

The pronunciation was not clear. It took me a moment to understand it and another moment to wonder what on earth he was doing in Cuba. Then it dawned on me. 'Was this… Guantanamo Bay?'

'Certainly it was. You know it? I stayed there for one year and one month.'

'What… was it like?' A pathetic question. But in a matter-of-fact way he described exactly what it was like.

'There were 48 cells, like this,' he demonstrated squares around a courtyard. 'Each room was ten forearm spans by eleven. They were made of wire and concrete and the weather was hot. There were 48 of us in this building.'

'Was the food bad?'

'The food.' He laughed. 'The food was small.' He slapped his thighs with both hands and laughed as if it had been some remarkable practical joke. 'It was so small. I am a Pashtun, I am used to bread like this,' he gestured a forearm length of the Pashtun roti, the largest size of flatbread in Pakistan. 'The Americans give us slices, like this', he piled his hands on top of each other, 'only two. Even double this would have been smaller than our bread. How can they eat such small bread?' Another laugh as if the real joke was on them with their pathetic loaf sizes.

'And the fish, in this Swat River that you can see under the bridge, the trout are the length of my elbow to my fist, but in Cuba the fish are very, very small. The smallest fish.' He pulled his chin in, incredulous that anyone could have such small fish and that even if they did they would have the cheek to serve it. They had imprisoned him but there was almost the sense in what he said that the Americans were the losers.

When I had left for Pakistan the newspapers had been full of the disturbing pictures of torture in the Abu Ghraib prison in Iraq. I asked him if he was beaten or tortured.

'No. The Americans did not beat us. I saw them beat the Arabs but that was because the Arabs spat at their faces. These Arabs are difficult men. Then they beat them. But they did not beat the Pashtuns.' He told me how he had come to be captured. They had crossed the border from Swat to Afghanistan shortly after the Americans had invaded. The Americans accused him of being Al-Qaida but he had not heard of Al-Qaida until he was captured. He never met anyone from Al-Qaida before Guantanamo. He had only gone because his cousins lived in Afghanistan and he could not leave them when they were being attacked.

'I went,' he said, 'for my family. I could not – not go. It would be impossible. I might as well put out my eyes.'

He was with thousands of other Pakistani fighters and it was only a few miles after they had left Pakistani territory by one of the numerous mountain passes that they were bombed from the air. Describing this part of the story was the only time he showed any emotion. 'Most of the men I went with were killed by the bombs,' he said and he set his mouth hard and turned his eyes away for a moment. 'My brother too.' Remembering it he exhaled through his mouth and muttered, 'Wah Allah.'

'But thanks to God I was not killed, only my hand was hurt and my eye.' He showed me the missing little finger on his right hand and the ragged scar running up the side of his hand and disappearing beneath the cuff of his shalwar kameez.

'The rest of us were taken prisoner and taken to Cuba where we were held for thirteen months. When we came back to Pakistan the police here arrested us and we were in prison for three months more. There the food is even worse. Then sent home, "*Challo Challo*," go.'

'How did your family live?' He had a wife and two young children.

'My family were OK. My father and my brothers cared for them.'

A moment of quiet. Then the question that had been bothering me. 'Do you hate me because I am from Inglistan?'

Another laugh, 'No I don't Ji. You are our guest.' He called to the *chaikhana* for tea. 'You are our guest and we will drink tea.' Several times in the following conversation he asked me to stay at his house – he had a guest room, I could stay for as long as I wanted, he said. It would be his honour. My sense was that he was a good man and he would do me no harm, but I had been warned about Swat and there was always the possibility that my intuition was wrong or that in a small village in this area the wrong kind of person could get to hear where I was staying. Part of me also wondered whether all of his story was true; I knew that the total number of inmates at Guantanamo Bay was fewer than one thousand and far greater numbers were interned locally. Possibly the story was a fiction or some less impressive story embellished with what he heard from others. I had no idea. In the end I chose the safe anonymity of a hotel.

In Mingora, the capital of Swat, I spent two days with Ajmal. Ajmal was two months older than me, an electrical engineer and the son of one of Mingora's tribal chiefs. When I first met Ajmal I began by speaking to him in Urdu but he asked me to speak in English.

'My Urdu is not very good, I never learned it properly. My university teaching was in English and my work is in Pashtun.' I had come across deficiencies in Urdu among uneducated people in the countryside, where in most cases it was the second language, but this was the first time I had seen it from a professional. It seemed to be another aspect of the famous independence of spirit of the Pashtuns.

Some parts of the Pashtun territory neighbouring on Swat are truly autonomous. The Federally Administered Tribal Areas are officially part of Pakistan, but the government has no direct control over them. These areas do not pay taxes and they essentially administer themselves. Problems arise when they start behaving in a way that the central government cannot tolerate. While I was in Mingora there was a week-long battle in Waziristan because a village was suspected of harbouring foreign Taliban fighters, including the then Al-Qaida number two, Ayman al-Zawahiri. Because the area had been left unpoliced the village was extremely well defended with mortars, RPGs and other heavy weapons. It took several thousand Pakistani troops over a week to secure the villages and fifteen died in the process. One hundred fighters were captured but al-Zawahari was not among them.

Mingora is not within the Federally Administered Tribal Area but Pashtun independence still showed itself in the area of law and order. There was a police force and a central legal system but these official systems were superfluous for the Pashtun community. The real controllers of law and order were the tribal leaders, men like Ajmal's father. They administered justice in the *jirga*, the tribal court.

Ajmal had a small apartment in a building next to his parents' compound. His parents' servants brought us lunch, passed in by a female servant from behind the door: aloo karai, bhindi, chapli kebabs, roast chicken, roti, chawal and yoghurt. It was delicious yoghurt.

'It is buffalo yoghurt.'

'Where do you buy it?'

'You do not buy it. We have our own buffalo. In the mornings the servants go to milk them and make the yoghurt. Go on, finish it, you will not find yoghurt like this in the bazaar.'

After lunch we watched the Bollywood classic *Kuch Kuch Hota Hai* then talked and smoked. The conversation turned, as it often did, to the Americans in Afghanistan. It was a conversation I have had before and as usual we agreed on some points and avoided others. Around this time the theory that the September 11 attacks of 2001 were a Jewish conspiracy had gained some ground in Pakistan. While such theories were quickly discredited they continued to circulate and Ajmal was convinced.

I changed the subject. This was 2004, some years before Osama Bin Laden was finally tracked down and killed about a hundred miles southeast of Mingora. At that point no-one knew where he was, although there were strong suspicions he was in Pakistan. 'Will they catch Bin Laden?' I asked.

'No.' Everyone said that.

'Where is he?' Normally the answer to this was a shrug followed by suggestions. Saudi? Islamabad? Washington with President Bush, his friend?

But Ajmal answered matter-of-factly. 'Today, I am not sure. But one week ago he stayed with the leader of the jirga nearby to here. You passed through this village on the way here. The thing is, he is safe here, and Pashtuns in Swat will not give him up because he is our guest. It is our duty to protect.' He paused. 'He is a jihadi…'

'If you told the Americans,' I suggested, 'you would get twenty million dollars.'

'It is true, but he is our guest.' He said this in a rather passionless way as if he were resigned to the annoying impediment of the Pashtun code of honour that stopped him becoming a multimillionaire. 'Guests are guests,' he said in a schoolmasterly voice.

'For example,' he turned his stoned, dilated pupils on me – 'I would not give you up for twenty millions…' He began emptying the tobacco from another cigarette and mixing it with charas to make another joint.

I changed the subject. 'Tell me how your father's jirga works.'

'If there is a crime, then the criminal and the man who is hurt go to my father's home. My father brings his uncles in and the families of the men and they all talk together. They decide what the criminal should have to do.'

'What kind of things?'

'Money. They would pay the man who is hurt some money. If it is a murder then they would have to pay the family and the murderer would be told to leave Swat for 25 years. He would have to go and live somewhere else, like Karachi.'

'Why do they not tell the police?'

'The police are not good. They take bribes and the man who is hurt gets nothing. If he gets nothing then he will want to take revenge and so the crimes will continue. The jirga stops revenge killings. This is why people like the system, because it makes an end. The Pashtun people need such a system, because, you must remember, we feel strongly.'

This last phrase seemed to sum up his people. These were people who were uncompromising in pursuing what they saw as honourable and right. Twenty-five million dollars, or the fingers of their hands, were secondary to this. They were stubborn. They felt strongly.

I remembered what I had read about the sentences passed by some jirgas that made families hand over daughters as wives, essentially slaves, in recompense for the crimes of a brother. It seemed medieval and unjustifiable no matter what crime had been committed. I mentioned this to Ajmal.

'This has happened in other places but it does not happen in the Mingora jirga. It is illegal.'

'What about a man from another town, or a tourist. If they were hurt would they come to the jirga?'

'No. It is for the families here. It only works because my father knows everyone. He knows how rich they are, how rich their cousins are, whether they are good or bad people.'

Ajmal would inherit a position on the jirga when he was older, but for now he found his position as the son of the jirga leader a bit of a burden. His father was angry with him, and had been for weeks, because he had found out about him smoking charas in his rooms. But he enjoyed smoking; why shouldn't he enjoy himself? He had once had a girlfriend, he told me. He had met her in Peshawar.

'How did you manage to meet a girl?' The segregation in Swat was even more extreme than elsewhere in Pakistan.

'She was in the same hotel. We saw each other in the morning and she looked at me. I knew she liked me. In the afternoon I stood outside all day so that she knew I was there and when she came back in she let her sister and mother go upstairs and she talked to me. I gave her my mobile phone number.'

It was quite an achievement, but Ajmal was tall and good-looking and he had the relaxed confidence that comes from being brought up wealthy. However, he would never be allowed to marry her because she was from an unsuitable family. His father told him he would marry one of the other jirga leaders' daughters, or maybe his cousin.

'I am like Adam Khan who loved Durkhanai.' He said this melodramatically and looked at me through glazed, stoned eyes.

I vaguely knew this folk tale. 'Tell me this story.'

There was a man who lived near to Mingora. His name was Adam Khan. One day while riding home from a business trip for his father he saw Durkhanai, the beautiful daughter of another tribal chief.

Their families were not friendly and there had been revenge killings between the two families. But Adam Khan had fallen in love with her and he could not think of anything else. He sat beneath a tree and thought only of the girl Durkhanai. An old musician met him as he sat beneath the tree and told him that he could attract the girl if he could play the rabab, the traditional lute-like instrument. But Adam Khan knew it would take him too long to learn how to play. The old rabab player was then shot – this is a Pashtun story, so no explanation is needed for this – and in a dream the old man came to Adam Khan. He told him to bury his body with the rabab, but said he could keep his *mezrab* (plectrum). After Adam buried the old man he found strings in the tree near the grave and from these he made a rabab. Using the old man's *mezrab* he found he could play perfectly as if he had been playing all his life.

Durkhanai was passing where he sat beneath the tree one day and immediately fell in love with him because of the way he played. They saw each other many times and she became his girlfriend. But their fathers would not let them marry and stopped Adam from seeing her. Both of them were kept locked up; Adam loved Durkhanai so much that he died from being apart from her. They buried him under a tree in a place called Bazdara. On hearing of this Durkhanai escaped her father and ran all the way to Adam's grave. When she saw it she was so sad that she died too. Then the families realised that their love had been so strong, stronger than anything, and buried the bodies together so that what they had not had while alive they could have when dead. Their families became allies. Now the two of them lie together and rabab players often go to Bazdara and take wood from the tree to make their *mezrabs*.

Ajmal ended the story by saying again, 'I am like Adam Khan.'

The story had spurred his imagination and that evening he asked his rabab-playing neighbour to come round. He was thin, with narrow, bird-like features. His tabla drum player came with him and we talked while he prepared his drum by laying a circle of fine clay on the centre of the skin. He rubbed at the edges of this damp circle to adjust the tone of the drum. The rabab player darted up and down the scale, tuning each of the five strings and beating at the sympathetic strings behind them to make sure the whole instrument was in harmony. He sang a song begging for spring to come to a high mountain village. His voice was thin but strong and as he sang it opened out. Several Pashtun love songs followed. Then Ajmal called for a Nagan. This word comes from the word for cobra, *nag*, and the racing tune of the Nagan with its repeating phrases and ever-accelerating rhythms is meant to be able to charm a snake. Ajmal beat his leg to the rhythm. For the final song, Ajmal asked for Adam Khan and Durkhanai.

It was a simple song. The tune danced but the vocal melody was simple. One phrase was repeated over and over, like a chorus. This was the phrase that Adam sang as he sat under the tree, then later played his rabab to, and at the end it was the song he sang from the grave.

'Please come, I am waiting for you, sitting here for you. Please come.'

'Please come, I am waiting for you, lying here for you. Please come.'

I looked across at Ajmal and saw wet lines of tears on his face. He said nothing but I remembered what he had said earlier about himself and the Pashtuns of Swat.

We feel strongly.

CHAPTER 7

DERAI AND TIRAT

The bakers fired up their tandoor at eleven and by quarter past they were hooking the first of the steaming rounds from where they had cooked, stuck to the curved interior of the oven wall. They wore turbans wrapped round their faces and heads to protect them from the heat. For an hour they sweated but by twelve, turbans off, they would sit by the cloth-wrapped pile of bread, drinking tea. It was best to get the roti so fresh and hot that they had to wrap it in newspaper for you, and it was still hot enough back at the hotel to melt the breakfast butter.

I was staying in a hotel in Madyan, two hours north of Mingora. From here I planned to cut over the mountain range to the neighbouring valley where the Indus ran alongside the Karakorum Highway and resume my route upriver.

Hot rotis in hand, I walked back to the hotel but on the way I was distracted by a crowd gathered round a man who was lighting a pile of charcoal by the side of the road. He called out, urging a bigger crowd to come and watch. Beside him a boy laid out rows of bottles and pots. '*Medicine, medicine, cures,*' he shouted. When a crowd had formed he drew them in closer, making the front row sit, and the back row close in shoulder to shoulder.

He broke a dozen eggs into a pot and scooped out the yolks with the palm of his hand to make a thick orange paste which he cooked solid in a small pan. He then squeezed the resulting omelette to make a thick black paste. All the time he did this he talked. I couldn't understand the details; he talked very fast and much of the vocabulary was technical, but he was explaining the various illnesses that would be cured by the mixture he was making. He gestured expansively to the rows of bottles, the bags of lichen and piles of seeds that his assistant had set out. He mimed the different infirmities while he talked about them, clutching his ankle, rubbing his back, squeezing his temples between his thumbs, rolling his eyes to signal pain – then – merciful, sweet relief. To attract attention and give him pause to think of his next dialogue he cried out a long call to the almighty, '*All-hahh*'.

He handed out oval seeds that looked like flattened chestnuts. 'Now break them in half,' he told the men who had taken one and the crowd laughed because they couldn't break the rock-hard seeds. He spotted some boys loitering at the edge of the crowd. 'Go now, go now. No children,' because the next part required some explicit explanation. He took the seeds back and added them to the bubbling mixture. He explained how this mixture not only cured bodily pains but also impotence. He stuck his index finger out, half straightened but still floppy. 'This is no good. This mixture will make it like this,' his finger shot out straight. With his left finger he held it down but it shot out straight again and the crowd roared with laughter. I lost track again as he explained the twenty other ingredients that he was adding. Some of them were potions, some were fibrous plants that flared and fizzed as they hit the boiling oil and egg extract. Each time, he told the crowd the Punjabi name for the ingredient and asked what the Pashtun word was. Some the crowd knew, others they didn't.

Now came the time to test it. The assistant poured the mixture between two pots to cool it.

'Who has some pain?' An old man who had been sitting at the front told him his leg gave him trouble. He rolled up his trouser to show thin white legs and the medicine man dropped the black mixture on to it.

'Rub it, rub it.' More men came forward and rubbed the mixture into their shoulders and necks and arms. The assistant decanted the cooling mixture into tiny plastic bottles. 'Any more pains and you should buy this. Remember Ji, what it can treat. It is truly a marvellous medicine. For men, All-hahh. This medicine made from 25 different cures is truly the best medicine for men. All-hahh. Only one hundred rupees for a bottle. God is great. It is not expensive. All-hahh.' The crowd formed a line. Only by buying a bottle could they rub it on themselves in private.

I told Fida, the hotel keeper, about the medicine man when I got back to the guesthouse. He snorted and called him a shopkeeper.

'He comes to valley to sell to ignorant men from the hills who think he is a Punjabi doctor. They think his bottles will help them with their wives. They will not. The real power-men are from Swat.' The men who make spells, he called them, the *mullasefs* – the teachers. 'They are the important men in Pakistan. They can see the future, they know things about what will happen to you. They can change the future. I have read in the newspaper that even our president Musharraf visits men like this. And our Benazir Bhutto also visited them to help with difficulties. I will take you to these men if you want.'

I had read about such men both in Pakistan and in Afghanistan where they are called *taweez naweez mulla*, fortune tellers or charm makers. But unlike in India where fortune tellers are easily found in the main markets, I had never met one in Pakistan.

So again my plans changed and I postponed my bus trip over to the next valley for a day so that I could meet the mullasefs.

We drove south along the steely waters of the Swat River. Eventually this water flows into the opaque Indus but up here it crashes over a bed of granite and it is clean enough to see trout in. At one point we stopped because Fida said there was an ancient statue in a field near the road, one of several in this valley. We knocked on the door of the nearest house and the farmer sent two of his children to guide us through the mud of the orchard.

'They have thrown stones at it. It is not so clear now.'

This had happened to so many of the carvings in the valley. Graven images, particularly of gods, are anathema to hard-line Muslims and they defaced statues. It was the same impulse or justification that led the Taliban to train their guns on the giant Buddhas at Bamyan in Afghanistan a few hundred miles west of here. They blew them up with dynamite when their guns proved too slow.

On a 4ft-high rock standing alone in the field I could just make out the shape of what looked like a seated man carved in relief but most of the image had now been obliterated. Looking at what was left I half wondered if it might be further evidence of the Shiva cult – the staff might have been a trident and the pose was certainly Shivaite, as was the long flowing hair. However, most statues in this area are

Buddhist, and this was likely to be too, although so little remained of it and it was so exposed that it would not survive much longer. Soon it would erode altogether and like the pre-Islamic magic of religious life in Pakistan, no-one would be able to quite remember where it had originally come from or what it had originally meant.

When we arrived to see the first mullasef, Asha Urstas, he was busy ministering to the women who sat in the next room. We waited on charpoys drinking tea while a man outside split green logs with an axe. It was like a doctor's waiting room. A man with two small, ill-looking children, a nervous old man with clouded eyes, young men talking in hushed, nervous voices. The tea tasted of wood smoke.

We heard chatter and saw the shapes of burqas move past the open door. The mullasef was now ready to deal with his male visitors. He wore an off-white turban and shalwar kameez. His beard was white, tinged with nicotine yellow at the end. He looked about eighty years old, and he shuffled with the help of a carved *darg*, a stick. He greeted each of us in the gentle Pashtun way, one hand on our back, the other on our heart, leaning in gently.

'*Salaam Alaikum.*'

'*Walaikum Salaam.*'

He leaned back on a pile of cushions and prayed, holding his hands open in front of him with his eyes closed. We all repeated his gesture. Visitors were brought to speak to him one at a time. He held their hands, nodded slowly at their answers and muttered prayers. The mullasef's son organised the sessions and wrote out the charms which the mullasef prescribed. He folded the charms into tiny squares and wrapped them in a self-sealed square of paper, folded in on itself. These charms would be sewn into a leather pouch and worn around the neck or the upper arm. In the Swat Valley most of the children had these tiny leather pouches around their necks, sometimes two or three on the same cord.

He came to us and Fida told him I would be interested in seeing his book of spells. It was worn and the cover had been rebound with cardboard and insulating tape. It was hundreds of pages of closely printed Arabic, sometimes interspersed with diagrams and matrices of magic arrangements of words. It was eighty years old, he said. Inside were loose-leaf pages of handwritten instructions which were even older, passed down the family line of mullasefs. He opened the book and explained.

'The come-hither spell:
Roll up the spell written as shown in the diagram and put it in your mouth between your gum and your cheek on the left-hand side. Press it, as they press the ball of naswar chewing tobacco, to get the full effects, and the person will come.'

'Stomach cure:
Make this diagram on a piece of paper, fold it and wear around the neck so that it is close to your stomach. The numbers have particular meanings and these were explained in another section of the book. Sixteen means God is helpful to me and knows what I have in my heart. One means God is enough for me and is my friend. Five means God is enough for me and is my counsel.'

After talking for a while with the mullasef in Pashtun, Fida told me, 'These spells all do good but there are some which you would call black magic. He does not give these out very much because it can cause trouble.'

This made me curious. 'Can he show me what a black magic spell looks like?'

'Charm to make two people enemies:
Write on a piece of birch bark paper the names of the two people and these words in Arabic. Then bury the paper between two graves.'

'The mullasef says you should not use this one. It is not a good thing to make enemies. He says he wants to give you something useful. Is there a spell he could make for you?'

'What kind of spell?'

'Any kind. What do you wish for? Many men of your age come here for one kind of spell.'

'Charm to make someone fall in love with you:
Make this diagram using these numbers in a grid. The numbers have various meanings: "*you love your Holy Prophet – you love your God – so much in love with God*." In the space at the bottom write your name and the name of the girl. Then fold it a square. Wear it round your neck but do not wear it if you go into any place where alcohol is drunk.'

Fida tied the knot behind my neck and tugged it tight. Then he pulled my collar up over the string and patted me on the shoulder. The way he did it felt like he was preparing me for a first day at school, preparing me to go out and achieve something important.

'This man has power.' He said to me quietly. 'You will see it will work…'

The second holy man was called, simply, 'the man from Derai'. He lived in a house painted light blue on the spur of a hill above the village. It started to rain as we arrived and we sat in his guest room and watched the staccato dimples on the stamped mud roof of the house below. There were several people waiting here, too. Some were farmers from Derai, still wearing their work clothes. Others looked much better off. One wore a pure white shalwar kameez, a symbol of his social station because it implied that the work he did wasn't the sort that would dirty his clothes. He had dark glasses and a large agate ring on his finger. He was a businessman from Mingora who had visited this mullasef some years ago when his business was in trouble. The mullasef had helped him and he was rich now but he continued to visit every month.

One of the farmers asked Fida. 'Who is this man with you?'

'He is a friend.'

'I know he is your friend – you arrived with him. But where is he from?'

'He is from the north so he does not have our tongue, but you know he has been working in Europe. Everyone needs to work and with the situation of our country at the moment you must understand that he has been working there. You would not blame him for this would you?'

'No, of course not. I too will go to Saudi Arabia to work.'

'There you go.'

The Man from Derai had a grey beard shaved at the moustache. His shalwar kameez was the colour of unbleached cotton and he wore a black waistcoat. The beard and the simple dress made him look like an Amish farmer. He wore a large turquoise stone inlaid with a silver star design and his right index finger was stained with henna up to the knuckle. He used the stained finger to point out the words as he read from his book.

The Man from Derai spoke to Fida and did not look at me.

'He is not from here.'

'No, he is from a nearby country.'

'Is he a Muslim?'

'No, Ji, he is not, but he has come far to see you; he wishes to write about this country and he is a good man and a polite man.'

The Man from Derai considered this for a moment and for the first time looked at me directly in the eye. He eyes took in my shalwar kameez, the blue Afghan lapis ring that I had bought in Peshawar, my shoes lying beneath the charpoy (tatty, but freshly polished on Fida's advice) and then back to my eyes. He nodded, still holding my gaze. 'All is well then. What is his name?'

'His name, uncle, is Iain Campbell.'

'Yeain Cambon, Yeain Cambon.' He scanned his text, running the hennaed finger along the lines of his book for clues to my future. The name was unfamiliar and he struggled to find the Arabic equivalent. He spoke in guttural Pashtun and Fida translated. The sentences came out with a sermon-like flow, steady, repeated and emphasised with an upraised stained index finger.

'You have many things in your mind. There are many things that you can do, but sometimes you are not satisfied with one thing and you are always changing your mind. You are always changing your mind. If you do decide to do one thing, one thing then you will be very successful. You can see so much. You want to spend time having fun – you like fun so much. So much fun... You are such a man that God never will give you a bad time and God will often give things to you very easily. The book that you will write will be both happy and sad. Some of the words are happy and others are not so happy. You will sometimes get so happy as you write it and at other times it will make you cry. Your book will be so interesting to you that sometimes you will want to do nothing else – but take care that you carry on doing the other things in your life. This is what I have to say for you Cambon Sahib.'

He turned to Fida. 'Fida Mohammed, Fida Mohammed,' he muttered while he sought the truth from the Arabic in front of him. When he spoke it was in a conversational manner, nothing mystical, as if he were talking in a tea shop about things that had happened rather than about things that would happen. He spoke to all of us about Fida. Privacy is far less valued in Pakistan than it is in the West but I was surprised that even the hidden future was not seen as something that should be private.

'Fida Mohammed, you are an honest man. You give food and tea to everyone. You show your heart to everybody. Better not to show quite so much from your heart. Do not share so much of your heart, just share your food and your tea. You don't have much money but everyone in your village thinks you have lots of money, even your brothers. I will give you my guarantee that you will always have food and will not have big problems in your life.'

Finally to the taxi driver. This time the speech was impassioned, motivational. I wondered why the deliveries varied so much for each of us.

'You understand so much more than taxi driving. You are a man with many abilities. Someone has offered you a visa for the Arab countries. You will get it in three months. You always worry about the money for this visa but you will find it when you need it. Do not worry, you will go. When you can go you must.' The delivery was persuasive, as if he knew the taxi driver was doubting the plan.

We thanked the Man from Derai and he called for his son who brought in a dish of honey that was so sweet it burned the back of my throat as I ate it. The comb hung in the honey and stuck in waxy pieces to my teeth, flavouring my whole afternoon.

The rain had stopped and the sky was clear. The rain had taken the cloying threat out of the air and the plants were washed clean. Brown streams ran in crumbling channels down the path from Derai village and at the road I could smell the steam that came off the tarmac.

In the evening I asked Fida how these men become mullasefs.

They do *pyawry kwl*, which means making strong. They go to a lonely place and repeat a special phrase over and over to themselves from afternoon until late at night. After a while spirits and fairies are called by these words and they circle the man. They appear in different shapes according to their characters. The better fairies are magnificent to see, they look like tigers and birds. The bad fairies look like men with horribly distorted bad faces. Big noses or faces that have sunk into their bodies so that their shoulders are at their ears and their beards hang down to their genitals. These spirits fight with the man and it is very difficult and exhausting. The man sweats and sometimes, if he is not strong enough, he will go crazy. They carry on shouting the words. It is this that makes a man a mullasef. Every mullasef must do this a few times when he is a young man, and strong, and then he will be able to use the power of the fairies for himself.'

'Where do they do this?'

'They must go to a place far away from any village. It is best at a V of land where two rivers join. Rivers bring fairies with them. They bring power and where two rivers meet is the strongest power.'

Once again it was rivers that delivered special powers.

I asked Fida how he knew all this and he told me he had attempted the process himself as a young man but the experience had put such heaviness on him that he could not continue. Besides, he would lose power from his occasional drinking of alcohol and his association with unbelievers.

'These men, once they have the power, must live very carefully and purely, not drinking or sinning in any way or their power will be lost to them. I could not do this.'

Fida was quiet for a few minutes. He looked into the empty tea cup in his hands and drew his knees up to his body.

'What he told me was true. The truth about what the people in my village think and what my family think of me. What he said of the taxi driver is true too. I know he will go to Saudi now. And what he said about you will be right too.'

I chuckled. 'I'm not sure the spell will work.'

'Ah, you are a doubting Thomas.' I heard the phrase frequently in India and Pakistan when discussing religion and belief, with its ironic Christian reference.

Like the shrine-focused Islam of Sindh, the religion of Swat was still coloured by a local pre-Islamic belief system. The fairies gave the power but the cures were delivered using the vocabulary of Islam – *you love the Holy Prophet, God is one*. 'Mullasef', the term which described these magic men, meant a sort of religious teacher, and the way in which they maintained their power was by living like a good Muslim man. But as with the Hindu beliefs it was water, and particularly river water, that brought the power, in a way that hinted at older beliefs.

In the villages further north around Chilas and Nanga Parbat I would hear about men who married fairies and talked to them.

Although it is very difficult to generalise about these things, I got the impression the Chilasi relationship with the fairies was more distinct from their religion. It was a slightly more guilty, pre-Islamic and mystic belief. In Swat the bond between magic, fairies and Islam was closer and, although at the periphery, the mullasefs seemed to be a semi-legitimate part of the religious structure. As I began to understand how the magic man and religion fitted together, the idea of the President of Pakistan visiting magic men seemed less remarkable. These were not occult practitioners, as their names suggested; they were almost mullahs.

On the way back Fida took me to the new mosque in Tirat. It had been funded, he told me, by a wealthy Saudi Arabian woman. The walls outside were clean, freshly painted concrete, and inside the floor was covered with quarter of an acre of new, machine-made carpets in green and beige. Vertical strip lights climbed up the internal pillars, highlighting the immaculate newness of the hall.

Two men wrapped in long khaki robes sat in the corner reading the Koran. Their faces looked foreign and when we left Fida confirmed that they were probably from Saudi Arabia and part of the Tablighi Jamaat, an ultra-orthodox Sunni missionary movement particularly active in India and Pakistan. 'They preach against what they call un-Islamic behaviour, praying at the grave-shrines of saints, making pictures of the caliphs, and visiting mullasefs. They want this to stop but they have a difficult job because in Swat we know that the mullasefs have power and we do not call it un-Islamic.'

Once again I was reminded of the wide spectrum of beliefs that exist within single religions. In this case it wasn't the division between Sunni and Shia but divisions within Sunnism. But now I had seen how important the mullasefs' role was in Swat I knew the Tablighi

Jamaat missionaries would have a hard task to wipe out these old beliefs. The complex of local beliefs that had grown up in Swat was like a tree that had grown into an iron fence and, over time subsumed its spikes beneath its bark. Something new had been created over decades and tearing the two apart would be traumatic and damaging.

The ground and fields around the mosque were muddy after the rain. The two robed figures had finished reading now and were looking out of the arched doorway, reluctant to leave its shelter. Their clothes were made for heat and dust, not for drizzle and mud and hand-ploughed fields. These men and their new cream-painted building looked unfamiliar and out of place in that little grey village of Tirat.

CHAPTER 8

KOHISTAN

From Swat I travelled over the Shangla Pass back eastwards towards the Indus Valley proper. As the minibus climbed we left behind the lush Swat Valley and inched our way up the switchbacks, the engine straining to keep going each time we slowed down to turn. Field terraces pushed the wheat fields as high up the mountains as they could go, but soon the ground was too steep and unstable to make terracing worthwhile, and our surroundings changed to the friable rock and scoured-out gulleys of the high mountains. A cold wind blew across the pass and we stopped to shiver and smoke before descending the other side, this time the engine straining to hold us back. By late afternoon we were low down again in the warmth of the valley at the small town of Besham, the last town on the Karakorum Highway route north before it entered Kohistan. I was headed for Aornos, 'The Rock', a mountain fortress on the west bank of the Indus that famously delayed Alexander the Great's sweep east, and weakened his army so much that it would only fight one more major battle. Rising from the plains and buckling into ever steeper mountains, the land here lends itself to defence.

The Rock lies on the southern border of Kohistan, an area which covers much of what was known to the nineteenth-century British authorities as Yaghistan, 'Land of the Ungovernable'. It remained an island of weakly controlled territory throughout the period. These valleys have also been the scenes of bitter inter-clan and inter-village warfare. As we drove along the Karakorum Highway I saw watchtower after watchtower, one or sometimes two in each village. They were dark and windowless and sloped up from sturdy foundation blocks so that they seemed to echo the spires of the cliffs above them. It was the land that directed how the Kohistani clans related to one another; the difficulty of communication between villages and the scarcity of arable land made for mutual suspicion and mutual aggression.

We know about The Rock from Greek historian Arrian's account of Alexander's campaigns; however, the exact location of the fortress was unclear until the early twentieth century when the explorer Aurel Stein made the journey that he later recounted in his book *On Alexander's Track to the Indus* (1929). The ascent of The Rock was the climax of Stein's journey. After several false starts he was told about a hill called Una that was similar to the description in Arrian's account. He described how he reached the ridge of Little Una and how the long, level ridge, girt with cliffs that dropped down to the Indus 5,000ft below, exactly matched Arrian's description. Although Stein reached the summit late in the day, his excitement was such that he continued along the snow-covered ridge to the ruined remains of a small fort. He was overjoyed to reach what he was certain was the fort of Aornos. 'I, too, felt tempted,' he wrote, 'to offer a libation to Pallas Athene [as Alexander had done on taking the fort] for the fulfilment of a scholar's hope, long cherished and long delayed.'

I wanted to follow Stein's footsteps to the fort on The Rock but I wasn't sure how. The best map I had was abstract and poor, as they are for most of rural Pakistan, consisting of only a few vague lines to mark Mount Una and Little Una. The names of the villages where Stein began his ascent had either changed their names or been abandoned. I knew it was near the village of Dandai but looking up from this village there were several possible peaks to choose from. It was clear I would need a guide, so I told the waiters in the Dandai truck-stop hotel that I wanted someone to show me the way to Mount Una, or Pir Sar as it is known locally, and sat down to tea and parathas. Dandai was a small place and I knew that word would spread quickly.

A gun-shop owner, in for his morning tea, told me Mount Una was very far away and very high and that there were men with guns there. 'I know because I sold them the guns.' Seeing that he had not been able to put me off, he sent me to see the bank manager, a man who ran a small micro-finance office, who talked to me about the state of the world, told me the Kohistan hills were not safe and asked me to help his friend the chemist get a visa in the UK. In return for my address he wrote me a note, as if his words written in English would have more emphasis than the advice he had already given me. He wrote it on a narrow piece of paper like a verse of modern poetry.

> *Your entry must in POLICE STATION*
> *Why you are foreigner*
> *The area is very difficults*
> *Mountains and Hard Area.*
> *There are no roads for*
> *Transporte you go by foot*

A bank customer arrived halfway through our conversation and said he would take me for a thousand rupees. I agreed to this and he left and returned with a boy – he had outsourced the job already. The boy had the look of a goat about him, a wispy chin beard, chipped teeth and a slow, confused gaze. I was not keen to take him; he looked lost already. The bank manager seemed to recognise my discomfort and scared the boy off by telling him all the terrible things that the police would do to him if anything bad happened to me.

Another boy approached me in the bazaar. He had an angular, pale face and curly, henna-dyed hair brushed in a wide side parting so that the curls sat high on the left side of his head. He had a thespian air about him and smelled of cologne. 'You want to go to Pir Sar, Ji. My father will take you, he knows the area and is an important man. You will be safe with him.' And that was how I met the wonderful Bachshar Zala.

Bachshar was a huge man with a semicircular beard that was intermittently streaked with henna where he dyed it to cover up grey hairs. He owned a shop in the bazaar that sold rice, flour, lentils and the cheap, tacky breakables that came down the road from China. There was a constant stream of visitors to the shop, and in between the greetings and embraces of the visitors we negotiated a guiding fee. With each visitor my confidence increased. The more important Bachshar was, the better. Often when I was looking for a local guide I would end up with the whole primary school class or one of the less capable adults with nothing better to do. If I was just trying to find a cave or a ruin, that was fine. But Kohistan was more dangerous than other areas and this guiding job more challenging. On this occasion it was best I went with a man of influence.

'Do you know the way?'

Above left: The fish market at Thatta, near the mouth of the Indus (page 11)

Above right: 'Thirty kay-jees of steel.' A Sufi holy man at the shrine of Abdullah Shah Ghazi in Karachi (page 18)

Below: The mudflats of the Indus delta – the starting point of my journey (page 5)

Above: Pollution and reduced river flow have greatly reduced the catch in Lake Manchar, but for these Mohana fishermen there is no other way of life (page 33)

Below: Devotional oil lamps at the shrine of Shah Abdul Latif in Sindh Province (page 24)

Above: Left to rust on its moorings, the *Indus Queen* is one of the many retired ferries of the Indus (page 68)

Below left: This wire bridge is the only connection with the outside world for this village in northern Pakistan

Below right: Fishing on the Gilgit River – one of the tributaries of the Indus

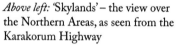

Above left: 'Skylands' – the view over the Northern Areas, as seen from the Karakorum Highway

Above right: One of the many elaborately decorated freight trucks that ply the Karakorum Highway from Pakistan to China

Below: Our first camp on the circuit of Nanga Parbat, the ninth-highest mountain in the world (page 121)

Above: 'I didn't know who would be waiting for us at the bottom. I thought I was through the worst.' The high point on the circuit of Nanga Parbat – Mazeno La (page 135)

Below: Katishoo village, the closest I got on the Pakistan side to the Line of Control (page 164)

Above left: Masked dancers at a Buddhist festival at Hemis Gompa, Ladakh (page 197)

Above right: The three-year-old Abbot of Mahe (page 207)

Below: Shopping by canoe – the floating market on Dal Lake in Srinagar (page 172)

Above: On the pilgrim trail to Amarnath cave with pack horses (page 177)

Below: The 'snake-encircled' temple – Likir Gompa in Ladakh (page 194)

Pilgrims making the ritual circuit of Mount
Kailash, the source of the Indus River (page 1)

'Yes I know the way.' His voice was deep and assured and he looked at me steadily as he spoke. 'The farmers who live up in the hills come to my shop and buy flour and dal. When they take the wool from their sheep I buy it. They are my friends and my customers. I go up to see them. I go up for business. But tell me Ji, why do you want to go up to Pir Sar?'

I told him that this was the hill where Alexander the Great, the warrior who is known in these parts as Sikander-e-Azam, fought his great battle that secured his rule over the area. The fort of Aornos, The Rock, was meant to be on the top of Pir Sar.

'Yes there are buildings there. Very old buildings.'

'A fort?'

'Maybe a fort but not much is left. Only rocks. We know the story of Sikander-e-Azam. He was a great man with much power. We are descended from him. That is why we are strong and good at fighting. Many men in the village are called Sikander.'

'Tell me about him.'

'He was a soldier. And a Muslim. He was a great man. Some say Sikander-e-Azam is still alive and that he fought next to the Prophet, peace be upon him. It was Sikander-e-Azam who drove the Hindus out. He was a jihadi.' Bachshar's history was confused. Alexander the Great was born around one thousand years before Mohammed and far from driving out religions he often incorporated the religious practices of those he conquered to further cement his territorial control. However, despite the shortcomings in his knowledge of history, I felt comfortable with Bachshar Zala. He was steady and trustworthy. My safety was further assured by his plan to bring his son along with us and the fact that his son would bring a gun. In the hills you have to be able to protect yourself. We would leave at dawn the next day.

It was a different son who came with us the next morning; the thespian was left to mind the shop. As soon as we cut away from the Karakorum Highway on to the track that led into the hills he put the pistol holster round his shoulder – for display, or for ease of access? We picked our way up a riverbed to begin with, and it was cool in the shadow. But as we climbed up the valley side the full glare of the sun hit us and the path got steeper. Sweat gathered on my temples and made drops at the end of my nose.

As we rested a group of men came jogging downhill carrying a quilt-covered charpoy on their shoulders. They called a hurried '*Salaam Alaikum*' as they passed and when they were beneath us on the next switchback of the path I could see the pale, unconscious face (it may have been a woman or a child) strapped under the quilts on the charpoy. Bachshar said one word: *bimar*, ill. There was no chance of help until they could get to the road. How awful, I thought, to have to endure several hours bumping down the mountain when already ill.

We climbed on through sculpted cultivation terraces that stretched above us in stripes of green corn and grey supporting walls. A man carrying an armful of corn sheaves led us up to his house and had his son bring us tea and water. He had a white beard that had been dyed months ago with henna so that now there was an orange stripe inches beneath his chin. He rested his sickle across his shoulder as he drank his pale, sticky tea, and I could see on the roughly sharpened blade the trapped sinews and fibres of the pale green corn stems.

From the flat mud roof of his house I could see the curve of the Indus shining like mercury in the high sun. It was this that protected the fort on the mountain above, as it meant it could only be approached from one direction. The haze that hung in the air caught the blue of the sky so that the mountains became flat shapes and far away they were just shadows.

Words of thanks were given for the tea.

'It is your kindness,' we said.

'The honour is mine,' he replied.

'Your hospitality, friend.'

'It is nothing, less than nothing. God go with you.'

'And you, Ji.'

Bachshar moved quickly, striding ahead with his chest puffed out and one hand holding the twisted knot of his blanket as it looped over his shoulder. Sometimes he bent himself forward and pushed himself up on his knees to climb up rocks in the path and then he would let out a mock-weary gasp and turn and smile at me. I kept up with him but it was as fast as I could go.

He paused, looking down. 'Our work means we must walk, Ji. I think yours does too.'

'My life means I must walk often, or at least now it does,' I replied in between deep gulps of air.

'Pashtuns like us are fine walkers. Strong legs are important for a man.' Then he boomed out to his son, who had paused to catch his breath on the switchback of the path beneath us, 'Come on – come on strong legs…'

As we moved between corn terraces he recounted who owned them, pointing out the houses and what relation, if any, they were to him or to each other. All of them he described as friends and in each case the friendship seemed to be related to his role as shopkeeper and sales agent or small-scale banker.

Three hours of walking brought us to the broad, grassy plateau where cows and goats were being pastured. Bachshar called out to a man sitting silhouetted against the sky. He stood up and walked to us. He was tall with an aquiline nose and a twirled Salvador Dalí-like moustache. He carried a Kalashnikov which had been elaborately decorated on the butt with patterns of stamped metal. His skin was darker than Bachshar's because he was a Gujar, one of the original Dardic clans who, so one theory goes, were pushed south and east or, in a few cases, pushed uphill to less attractive grazing areas by the arrival of Aryan Pashtuns from the west. There were two hundred Gujars on Pir Sar. On a neighbouring higher hill was another Dardic clan who tended to migrate even higher by only herding goats. The Gujar man pointed out their lowland village, which he called Chat. They lived there in the winter. Stein mentioned this village as the starting point for his climb, but I had been unable to find it on any maps.

The Gujar now accompanied us along the ridge. The cows had cropped the grass bowling-green-short and children ran among the animals playing with homemade catapults. The older ones herded the cows or carried water back from pools that were fenced off to stop the animals polluting them. All the men we passed were armed, most with antique-looking rifles although a few of them had automatic weapons. The ridge narrowed to a rocky slope. We climbed over boulders and across fallen pine trees and finally reached the crumbling walls of the old fort.

There was not much left of it, and it was overrun with trees and undergrowth, but I could just make out five separate rooms. I sat on the highest wall and looked down past the steep natural fortifications of Pir Sar to the Indus far below.

As Alexander advanced, the inhabitants of Bazira retreated to The Rock but continued to attack the army as it passed through the narrow valleys approaching the fort. Alexander's army was huge and it easily reached the base of Aornos, but could go no further. The flattened ridge could support livestock and crops and there was fresh water, which meant Alexander could not starve the defenders out. He chose to assault from the north where a neighbouring peak gave enough elevation for catapults to be effective, but bombardment alone could not take the fort. Alexander was finally forced to build a bridge between the two mountains, filling up the ravine between them with earth and trees held together with a wooden structure. It took his army three days to build the mountain far enough out to reach a lower hill connected to Pir Sar. The defenders rolled boulders on to Alexander's men but could not defend their position for long and three days later Alexander had captured the fortress. On the summit he erected altars to Athena Nike and offered libations to the gods.

Looking down from the ruins I could see the narrow earth ridge stretching away to the north. This was what Stein identified as Alexander's earth causeway. In battles on the plains his huge force (built partly from defeated armies) and his tactics allowed him to sweep east so successfully. But up here in Kohistan Alexander had been forced to change the very topology of the land in order to conquer its inhabitants.

After Aornos, Alexander had one more major battle to fight against the army of King Porus at the Battle of the Hydaspes River in what is now the Pakistan The Punjab. But then his army refused to go further; Arrian reports that one of the veterans advised him, 'Sir, if there is one thing above all others a successful man should know, it is when to stop.' Alexander could not drive on an unwilling army, so on the banks of the Indus he picked men from seafaring nations – Phoenicians, Cypriots, Egyptians, Indians and Hellespontines – and instructed them to build a giant fleet to transport his army home. Arrian puts the number of ships at two thousand.

Stepping aboard, he [Alexander] stood in the bows of his vessel and from a golden bowl poured a libation into the water, solemnly invoking the river… its tributaries… and, finally, calling upon the Indus too… ordered the trumpets to sound the signal for departure, and the whole fleet, each vessel in her proper station, began to move down-river.

Arrian *The Campaigns of Alexander* (trans, Penguin 1971)

It was on the banks of the Indus that Alexander decided to bring an end to his military conquest and turn towards home. He would not make it back, however, and died aged 33 in Babylon.

We thanked the Gujar men for taking us to the fort – the thanks were elaborate again – and then rather than retracing our steps we kept going along the extended ridge of Pir Sar so we could look back on the fortress of The Rock from the side that Alexander approached from. The track descended in long zigzags, cutting round the steep defiles of stream beds. We passed a line of five men, the males of a family, each one carrying a sack on his shoulder. '*Ta sanga yee,*' the youngest at the front piped, the Pashtun greeting. '*Ta sanga yee,*' each one repeated with gradually deepening voices until the bearded father at the back clasped Bachshar to his chest with his free hand and poured out greetings. He didn't let go of Bachshar's hand and pulled him with him, insisting we climb back up with him to take tea in his house. Bachshar excused us; the host pressed him again but eventually relented and sent us on with blessings. At the next house the farmer pulled us in and gave us each a bowl of goat's cream which we scooped up with thick cornflour chapattis followed by glasses of sweet milk tea.

It was getting late, we had been walking for eight hours, and the food made me tired. My legs felt old and slow and there was a residue of sweat covering my clothes and skin so I felt like I had been wrung out. The men were back from the fields and sat in groups at the doors of the houses. They called out to us as we passed, demanding we come to drink tea, or eat their evening meal with them, or sleep the night in their homes. During the climb up there had only been women at home and if they were working outside they turned away as we passed, hastily pulling their veils around their heads. Bachshar and his son walked quickly around these houses in quiet respect of their modesty. There were few reasons to stop on the way up, but now on the descent each house required five minutes of conversation. We always said we were too full to eat and would just have some water. But as we drank there always appeared a dish of spinach or dal from the dinner pot, so that the stop lasted longer than intended.

We passed through a valley that had recently been cleared of all its trees by loggers so the ground was covered in sawdust and offcuts. We lost the path under the debris and the ground fell away towards a river. We clambered down over shelves of rock and splashed along its course desperately looking for signs of the path. Then we emerged into terraced fields again and saw that we had left the path behind above us, skirting the flanks of the mountain.

The sun fell; we had left Besham twelve hours before. I wasn't sure which way the road was but Bachshar and his son knew the paths and I kept close behind them. Lights came on in the houses and back and forth across the valley came the barking of dogs. Now the houses were shut up and the people had vanished from the valley. When we saw a house ahead we climbed high above it because the guard dogs were dangerous at night. During the day they were tied up, harmless and timid, but at night they barked blindly at the sound of our footsteps and bounded towards us. In an hour the valley had changed; before we had been slowed down by hospitality and now we were hurried on by growls in the dark. Bachshar gave me stones to throw in case a dog attacked us.

We paused after a deep river crossing to empty our shoes and Bachshar spoke. 'No-one walks at night. It is dangerous, but unfortunately we must go on because I told the police that you would be back today. If it were not for the police I would sleep now in a friend's house.'

'When did you tell the police?'

'They asked me yesterday.'

I had made my plans fairly well known in Dandai and I shouldn't have been too surprised to find that my plans had filtered back to the police station. I hadn't registered with the police because I was concerned they would prevent me from going.

'What did the police say?'

'They did not want you to go. I told them I would fool you and take you to a mountain close to here and tell you it was Pir Sar. But we were going fast so we went all the way. I had forgotten the path back was so long. It is maybe one more hour, but we must go carefully. It is not far but it is not good to walk at night. The people do not like it. Only robbers and bad men walk at night. There are dogs and the farmers will be scared. If someone shouts at us I will speak. Stay close and walk quietly.'

At the next house Bachshar stood at a good distance and called out. The conversation was long and when we approached the farmer was hesitant and cautious until he was sure it was Bachshar. They spoke together in Pashtun, then Bachshar turned to me. 'The farmer says we should not go on. He says we should stay with him tonight but I have told him we must go back to Dandai. He will come with us because we are passing his brother's house and his wife's brother's house lower in the valley and they might shoot us if he does not come with us.'

We didn't stop for tea. The mood of the walk had changed; no-one liked being on the road in the dark. Not in Kohistan. Not in Yaghistan. Even the confident Bachshar was nervous now, and I was worried that I had got us into trouble. The weather turned, too. A wind was bending the trees and from behind us came the muffled bass of a storm. The wind blew the rain in quickly and we pulled our blankets over our heads and stumbled on. In some ways the weather was useful as the dogs couldn't hear or smell us above the storm. Very soon I was completely soaked and my blanket lay in heavy folds around me. Bachshar's beard was drenched and stuck together in strands like seaweed. His face was greasy with the rain and he was breathing through his teeth with his cheeks pulled back as if in pain.

With the road finally visible we sheltered in a half-built house, shivering as we said goodbye. Bachshar took the farmer from up the valley to stay in his house just outside Besham while his son put the pistol under his shalwar kameez and walked me to the truck-stop hotel where we ate bowl after bowl of dal mash and chapatti. The pistol was clearly outlined beneath his soaked shirt but there was no-one to notice now. Trucks normally drove through the night and gave the hotel plenty of visitors but in heavy rain, rock falls were likely and the Highway would be quiet for the night.

Without his father there he talked more. He told me how he had not wanted to walk in the dark. How it was a really stupid thing to do. How he had never made the thirteen-hour round trip to Pir Sar before – normally there was business to be done and they would sleep at whatever house they arrived at in the evening. He laughed about something funny the Gujar had said about his cows. Gujars are said to be very fond of their livestock and particularly their cows. 'They are strange men.'

'Do you ever sleep in their houses?'

'No.' They would stay at any Kohistani Pashtun house but never at the Gujar settlements. Likewise there was no intermarrying between these different people although the Gujars would sometimes intermarry with other nomadic herding tribes. 'Or their cows!' Bachshar's son doubled up with laughter and called the waiter over to hear the joke.

I left Besham the next morning, heading north on the Karakorum Highway. I had been up and down it many times already in preparation for this trip. I remembered the first time very clearly, when I had taken a night bus and had tried to sleep. For twelve hours I had rested my head against a headrest that jolted so much that my teeth felt loose in the morning. This time it was a grey day and still spitting. I didn't like travelling on the Karakorum Highway in the rain when it loosened the sides of the valleys, but I wanted to get up to Gilgit where I could rest. My legs were stiff from thirteen hours of walking and I felt I was developing a cold.

We crawled up the valley, passing the heavy lorries with their wheezing hydraulics and groaning gearboxes. These trucks were strange hybrid machines. Their panels were immaculately painted with peacocks and flowers and chrome filigree, but beneath the pristine metalwork were creaking axles and dirty exhausts.

Attached to the middle of the bus windscreen were strings of coloured beads that swayed and jolted with the road. When we were stationary two of the shorter strings jumped in tune with the engine but the rest hung vertically and the pattern of writing coalesced into clarity – in swirling Arabic writing, *Allahu Akbar*.

Beyond Besham the pine trees thinned and were replaced with clumps of scrub bushes that clung to the scree and cliff. The river here was silted an opaque grey, carrying down the dust and the stones with its force. Where there were gaps in the cliffs above a track would meander down from the high ground. At the junction with the Highway there was often a truck stop, a few charpoys and piles of square-cut logs brought down from the forests above. These stops smelled of grit and the kerosene stoves that kept the tea hot. Behind the tea shacks were the latrines and beneath them scree runs of dried shit and rubbish running down to the river. Once I saw a Jeep-truck taxi clatter down one of these tracks, overbalanced-looking with a dozen men standing on the back. They all had long beards and long noses beneath their folded Chitrali caps. You didn't go into the higher valleys without being invited; these were among the most conservative and closed communities in Pakistan, where 'Land of the Ungovernable' was still an accurate description. As we drove through this desolate area I asked the man next to me the name of each valley and he accompanied the name with his view of their safety. There were three rankings, *xatarnak, bahut xatarnak, band*: dangerous, very dangerous, closed.

When the Indus Valley slopes grew temporarily gentler small settlements appeared, their boxy houses forming steps upwards until they reached impassable cliffs. What few windows these houses had were tiny and dark, no more than a brick-shaped gap in the blank defensive walls that faced the road. The landscape grew more barren and inhospitable as we drove north and apart from their goats these villages had no obvious means of survival. Only rarely would I see flashes of colour as children played cricket or flew kites from the flat roofs of these monotone fortresses.

Then the valley tightened, the sides became steeper and steeper and the world felt like it was being folded up. The towering slopes here soared hundreds of near-vertical feet above the road and were uninhabitable; even the scrub could not cling to the ground anymore. The cliff was grey and the scree was grey and the road was dust and it felt as if we had landed on some distant waterless planet. The river cut through bare rock and the road did the same, burrowing into the mountain in tunnels when there was no other way through. Rubble piled on either side of the road, where it had been recently cleared like a snowdrift, temporarily claimed back from the mountain. When the rocks fell in the channel here they were washed down with the power of the water and sometimes as we sat in a teahouse we could hear the rumble of these underwater rolling boulders. They call the Indus Aba-Sind here, the 'father of rivers', because it is here that it seems to emerge energised from the mountains.

Before the Karakorum Highway opened in 1979 it was impossible to travel all the way up the river valley and the main path north cut away from the river across the hills into the Swat Valley before re-crossing higher up and following precarious tracks cut into the cliffs to go east. The Chinese traveller Fa-Hien in the fourth century described the upper route:

The road was difficult and broken, with steep crags and precipices in the way. The mountain-side is simply a stone wall, standing up 10,000 feet. Looking down, the sight is confused, and on going forward there is no sure foothold. Below is a river called Sintu-ho. In old days men bored through the rocks to make a way, and spread out side ladders, of which there are seven hundred in all to pass.

> From *Fo-kwo-ki*, quoted in George N Curzon,
> *The Pamirs and the Source of the Oxus* (1896)

Only dynamite, pneumatic drills and the constant attention of the Pakistani army engineering corps, often with assistance from Chinese engineers, have made this valley passable and thereby created a direct trading link between Islamabad and Chinese Kashgar.

We emerged from the rock-funnelled river of Kohistan into the district of Chilas. The cliffs retreated slightly and we drove through a desert of mica sand and black obsidian. While the people in Chilas looked the same, their headgear was subtly different: as across most of northern Pakistan and much of Afghanistan the men here wore folded wool Chitrali caps, but in Chilas the upper part of the hat was broader so that the top extended beyond the sides like a French beret.

Darkness came and after the exertions of the previous day I couldn't stay awake, but the jarring of the road wouldn't let me sleep properly either. What went on around me felt like a dream and I observed it as if from a great distance. The bus braked suddenly and a man was carried aboard. He groaned as he was laid on the seat behind me and pleaded not to be touched anymore. I woke up in Gilgit. We were at the hospital, and I realised the man on the back seat had been run down somewhere back on the Highway. His shalwar suit was torn and his shoulder was covered in blood from a gash on his head.

The police attendant tried to pull him out by his legs and the man came out of his unconsciousness and shrieked. They collected a stretcher and took him inside.

I fell asleep again in the ten-minute drive to the centre before stumbling through the unlit alleys to the welcome quiet of my favourite hotel in Pakistan.

CHAPTER 9

NANGA PARBAT

Gilgit's Madina hotel was where I rested; a sort of base camp of familiarity. I had come to the Madina for a fortnight at the beginning of my journey to turn my book-learned Urdu into Urdu that I could actually communicate with. Months later I would come back to Gilgit from India and start laying down the outlines of my book at the chipped white tables in the shaded courtyard of the Madina.

Each time I arrived at his hotel Yaqoob embraced me and called for tea. I had met Yaqoob in 2002 on my way through western China. He had travelled north to Kashgar because in the wake of the invasion of Afghanistan there were no tourists for his hotel and Yaqoob had begun to miss their company. He also wanted to solve the problems that were affecting his business and his solution was to send a letter of advice to President Bush. 'I will write it out neatly and put it inside a card of the mountains,' he told me. 'I think he would like such a picture. Maybe it would make him read it. The problem is my English, which is, excuse me, not so good. Maybe you can help?' He gave me a blank sheet of paper and I copied out his letter to George Bush, correcting the spelling and grammar and consulting Mr Yaqoob on word changes as he sat there, his brows still furrowed, sipping milk tea. I was half amused at what he wanted to write, but Yaqoob was so serious about it that I didn't even smile. He worried about the advice he was giving as he worried about everything else in the world; the Indian nuclear tests, the prospect (then) of a war in Iraq, the fact that the Chinese smoked so much. He seemed to seek out problems that he had no hope of finding a solution to in order to worry about them. His stumbling gait, unsteady hands and his clouded left eye seemed almost to be symptoms of this self-consuming anxiety. But he was also a deeply kind man and he became a good friend.

Mirza was Yaqoob's business partner but his character was quite different. Yaqoob's anxious innocence made him one of the worst business minds I have come across, and he always seemed to be running from one cash crisis to another, often as a result of giving handouts to penniless tourists or relatives. Mirza was more worldly-wise and had a cooler temperament. They were an effective team – Yaqoob welcomed guests and overburdened them with tea and greetings, while Mirza smoked Capstan after Capstan all day and offered seasoned advice on cheap Jeeps going north, or how to jump the queue for the overbooked flight to Rawalpindi. Mirza was also tall, good-looking and charming. On my return to Pakistan this year, I found that he had recently married a Korean structural engineer who had fallen for his charms on her way up the Karakorum Highway and had flown back from Taipei to be with him. Mirza was also a mountain guide and he had agreed to take me on a circuit of Nanga Parbat.

For the first six hundred miles of its course the Indus flows northwest, caught in the giant northwest-sloping furrows of the Himalayas. In the Karakorum at last it can swing south, and the final mountain that is the axle of this swing is the ninth-highest mountain in the world, Nanga Parbat, which, loosely translated means 'Naked Mountain'.

I wanted to walk round it, from Indus to Indus, starting near Astore higher up the river and climbing up over the high glacial passes before descending back to the river valley at Raikot Bridge.

We crossed the Indus and began a juddering drive up the incomplete road to Astore. It was slow-going and we passed teams of road makers variously engaged in mixing concrete, drinking tea, quarrying, praying and dozing. They waved as we passed with the multipurpose word '*Syo*', which means 'good' in the Shina language, but in the Chilasi dialect seems to be used for OK, I agree, goodbye, hallo and so on.

The outer ridges of Nanga Parbat stretch out like the thirsty roots of some giant tree and as we approached the mountain we drove over these elongated spurs on gear-crunching switchbacks before freewheeling down the other side, sending up dust trails. We roared through tiny settlements huddling in the dips of valleys and crossed channels which flowed with a thick mix of meltwater. We were getting close but still the foothills obscured our view of the snow.

In Astore, the last town big enough to have a market, Mirza had a panic that the four hundred cigarettes packed in our supplies might not be enough and we searched the bazaar for a third carton. Then we were back on the track again and I could almost feel the wind through the window get colder as we approached the valley beneath the north Rupal face.

It was astonishing to see it in front of us suddenly. The Rupal face is the largest mountain face in the world, 15,000 vertical feet high and 12 miles long. On that clear July day in the pure, high atmosphere, each runnel and ice-crusted steeple seemed to be etched out in high definition. The face took up my whole field of vision so that I had to move my head to see its entirety. First I ran my eyes along the vertical crimpings of the drawstring summit ridge. I had to focus and refocus to trace the miles of undulating snow slope. I had to turn away and look back again to absorb with fresh eyes the afternoon-reflected light and the way its low angle made one side of the descending ridge black and the other side bright yellow, with the ridge itself as sharp and freshly defined as a trouser crease. It was huge and dramatic, but it was also covered with detail: the flecks of rocks and filigree gullies, the shattered faces traced with frost. Like a huge tapestry, each inch filled with detail. Like the skin of an ancient sea mammal.

I watched it as we drove closer to it, then I watched it in the hotel garden while Mirza drank tea and talked loads and stages with the porters. I followed each ridge up, traced the snowless slabs and wondered at the speed of the wind at the top where it sent a streamer of spindrift hundreds of feet into the air. The streamer curved up then drifted down in a widening, blurring line to make soft, rolling drifts on the western face.

How could these men cutting the ditch in the field bear to ignore it for a second? How could Mirza go inside and talk business when the Rupal face was out here? I lay against the wall and drank in the scene for hours.

Nanga Parbat's name, the 'Naked Mountain', is a reference to the black main summit which is too steep to hold snow. Early European climbers called it the 'Killer Mountain', because of its terrible reputation for disastrous expeditions. The first serious attempt on the summit was made by the legendary English mountaineer A F Mummery in 1895. He initially climbed from the west and reached 20,000ft but failed to summit. While reconnoitring the Rakhiot face in preparation for another attempt, he and his two Gurkha companions were caught in an avalanche and killed. The mountain had claimed its first climbers.

In 1932 a German–American team failed to reach the summit but all the team members safely made it off the mountain. On the voyage back, however, during a stopover in Egypt, one of the climbers fell to his death off the Chefren Pyramid. With this event began the reputation of the mountain as having malevolent powers or being somehow cursed.

In 1934 another German expedition set off with the leader Merkl announcing, 'We must succeed at all costs'. 'And what if you are not successful?' 'Then I won't come home!'[4] Big mountains in those days were climbed using siege tactics, which involved large teams shuttling equipment and provisions to increasingly high camps on the mountain. It was partly because of this style of climbing that sixteen men came to be camping at 24,540ft on the mountain in an increasingly ferocious storm. The storm lasted two weeks and nine of the men died, including Merkl himself.

Another expedition set off in 1953 and the summit was finally reached by the audacious gamble of a single Austrian climber,

---

4 *The Naked Mountain: Nanga Parbat – Brother, Death and Solitude* by Reinhold Messner (English translation, Crowood Press, 2005).

Hermann Buhl, pepped up on the amphetamine Pervitin. He very nearly became another victim of the mountain – had it not been for freakishly calm weather he would not have survived the cliff-bound standing bivouac at 26,000ft that he was forced to endure during his descent. The strains of his climb were such that as he was descending Buhl hallucinated that he was accompanied by other climbers, and although he continued to take amphetamine pills he fell asleep in the snow on several occasions. This success story has a sad epilogue as some years later Buhl was killed on Chogolisa, a mountain to the northeast of Nanga Parbat.

Local people call Nanga Parbat '*Diamir*', the fairy stronghold, because it is on the high ridges of the mountain that they say the fairies live. Mirza said, when I asked him about this, 'They hate the loud noises that we make with cars and blasting machines and so they have left the places that they used to live in and have all gone to live in the stronghold.' He said it with a smile.

'Do you believe that?' I thought he was just repeating the myths to amuse me. I didn't expect Mirza to be the superstitious type; in every other way he was so modern and literal.

'You know there is something true in these stories actually. I can say this with certainty.'

'Tell me, then.'

'I will tell you. I know so many. We have many days walking to go so this is what we will do. Each day we will walk and in the evening I will tell you the stories about the fairies. Up in these mountains where the roads don't go, things work differently. I think you will hear some surprising things.' He still smiled a bit, and I wondered if he was just doing his duty and adding local colour. But maybe these things could only be said with a smile when we were still so close to the road.

So that was what we did. In the morning we woke early and walked while it was still cool. When we reached camp we set up the tent, changed our socks and sat back in the sun with the strong Capstan cigarettes, the only brand Mirza would touch. Then Mirza would tip his cap over his eyes and look out at the glacier and tell me stories while the porters cooked the meal.

From Tarashing we walked west beneath the Rupal face for three full days up the tightening Rupal Valley. Rupal village was surrounded by the white-green stalks of unripe barley but it was a ghost town. Every house was well maintained but shuttered up, as the inhabitants were at their lower village handling the harvest of their lower-altitude crops. To spread the demands of work each community had a lower-altitude and a higher-altitude village which they populated alternatively depending on the season.

I walked on ahead fast and perspiring happily. For the first few days the path was flat enough for the porters to load their sacks on to a donkey and Sher, a broad, bearded Choriti, walked behind the donkey prodding at it when it slowed. When it went up a slope Sher was level with the donkey's rear end and it farted with the effort. I looked at Sher, smiling, ready for a joke, but he was used to it and had clearly long ceased to find it amusing.

The sun rose higher and the Rupal face lost its yellowed textured surface, turning bleached and flat in the midday light.

My feet had worked through their twinges, every potential discomfort notifying of its presence, a roll call of potential blisters – right foot, little toe knuckle; right foot, heel left side; left foot, big toe two-week old stubbing bruise… and so on. But now they had made their complaints and they settled down to work quietly.

By lunchtime we were at the Helicoffer base camp. It was also known as the Japanese base camp and the Polish camp. The camps took their names from the dead, changing to the nationality of those most recently buried. It had been a gentle first day. I lay against my pack, facing the mountain, and watched the slow-motion plumes of ice dust rise from the high corries as cornices collapsed into them. While I watched, Mirza told me a story about a group of young climbers who had annoyed the fairies of the mountain by playing loud music at their base camp. They ignored the rock falls that came down near their camp although their porters warned them that this was a sign the fairies were angry with them. After one particularly raucous night they woke in the morning to find that an avalanche had swept their climbing gear, stored in a pile of blue barrels, into the river. Their tents were untouched and no-one had even heard the avalanche in the night. They had to abandon the route and go home.

Day two: up at 4:30am for the obligatory dawn-light photograph of the Rupal peak washed in pink light, taken bleary eyed from the door of my tent, then back to sleep until six. It was another easy day. The only real climb was in the first hour, up the lip of a ragged, messy glacier. My boots crunched on the gravelly ice and beneath I could hear the whispers of submerged rivers. Where the gradient of the rocky substrate changed beneath the glacier, the ice arched up into dirty fins and spires that melted in the sun and seeped into green pools.

Farmers brought donkey-loads of firewood down to their villages and we stepped aside for the donkeys to pass; they were not aware of how wide their loads were and could easily knock us off the crumbling glacier paths.

We camped at Latobah on springy turf beside a stream. It had been a short day and we arrived at lunchtime. Over the afternoon the sun warmed up the glacier and the stream that ran from it changed from clear water to brown soup. The porters suggested we buy a goat here to slaughter near the pass to ensure our safe passage, so we walked up to the village to look at the animals.

Although this village was high it was inhabited all year round, unlike the seasonal villages we had passed. The walls of the houses were earthed up with dung, I guessed for insulation and the heat that it gave off, but it meant that the only way in to one of the houses was down a ladder through a hole in the roof. The porters asked around for a goat but none of the animals was for sale – which was a bit of a relief.

Back at the camp we lazed. Mirza told me that the valley was said to be rich in gold, scraped down from the mountains in the glaciers. In between cups of tea and Capstans I tried to pan for gold but everything sparkled with mica and the mud washed in with the water obscuring the sediment. I slowly read my book. I only had one with me, to last for two weeks, so I had rationed myself to twenty pages a day.

The sun rolled down and the snow fields steamed in the afternoon heat. Sher picked through the lentils to remove the stones and as the melting sun strengthened, the river ran thick like chocolate. Mirza told a story:

'The people who live by this mountain believe that in the afternoon when the mist rises from the snow, this is the fairies baking their bread. Every day at the same time they have to bake their bread just like us. There is a story from my village that there was once a very good farmer who was an expert in doing the repairs on the village mill. One day, soon after his third son was born, he disappeared from the fields where he had been working. His fields were close to the mountain but there had been nothing dangerous there, no storm or avalanche, and although the villagers searched hard they never found any footsteps or body. Then one day a fairy came to one of the old people in the village (who was known to have some contact with them) and told him that they had taken the farmer and that he was now grinding flour for them and helping to keep their mill going. His family gave up on his ever returning but his sons used to watch the smoke rise from the mountain in the afternoon and they took comfort that he was still so skilled and was helping to bake so much bread. Sixty years after he disappeared the fairies told the wise man in the village that the farmer had recently died at the age of 106 but that he had worked very hard and they were very pleased with him. At this news the sons, who were now old men themselves, held his funeral.'

The next day we walked above the Rupal glacier, white and grey and brown in swirling lateral furrows. Somewhere beneath the broken ice the glacier met the mountain and ground it slowly away.

There was a dead yak calf at the next camp. It was recently dead – its eyes had gone but its tongue still lay plump over dry teeth. Its stomach had been slashed open by a bear but the body was otherwise undamaged. It must have got separated from its herd in the night because it seemed that the rest of the herd had only just discovered the body as we arrived. The older yaks were agitated and bounded around the body like giant mastiffs with their tongues out, bellowing.

They licked the dead calf on the ears and neck and around the wound on the open ribs. After this some of the young bulls became angry and butted one another, sending dust into the air and the stones flying from their scraping hooves.

The big bull of the herd came last to the calf – a hazel beast, shaggy like a yeti and full shouldered so its head hung far beneath its body. Sher proudly told us that along with the rest of his community he was a part-owner of this stud bull. We made camp some distance up the slope where some large boulders made a natural shelter. Mirza told another story:

'All the animals that live in these valleys, the yak and even the bear, are scared of the high slopes because there is a huge she-snake that lives in the snow. Once every ten years she calls to her mate who lives in one of the Kohistan lakes. They go to meet each other in a high lake and on the way there they cause terrible destruction, ripping up trees, flattening fields of barley, knocking down houses and killing animals as they slide their huge bodies along the ground. When they get to the lake their spinning bodies make the lake boil. They do this at night. The fairies prepare the route and it is important you do nothing to annoy them, like making a loud noise or using their glaciers as a toilet. If you do this they will guide the snake through your property and there will be terrible destruction.'

Mirza had delivered the story in a stern voice, almost as a warning, and the two porters nodded earnestly when he summarised it for them in Urdu. We looked down the hill towards the carcass of the dead yak.

'This animal though, I think it is killed by a bear, not the snake. The snake would have caused much more damage. Tonight we must wrap our food carefully and put it far away from our camp, and we must make the fire smoke a lot to scare away the bear.' Mirza chuckled as he picked up tiny pieces of dung from the grass around the camp and tossed them into the fire where they sizzled and steamed. 'The bears hate the smell of smoke,' he puffed on the Capstan drooping from his lips and grinned. I glanced back at our little tent in the crevice of the rocks; it seemed strange to me at that point that the bear was being taken less seriously than the fairies.

The next day the weather closed in. Dark clouds washed down to hide the mountain and the air was wet with mist. We left the yaks in the valley and began the two-day climb to the Mazeno La, the high pass of the circuit. Gradually, as we walked, the ground grew less and less fertile. The grass thinned to spiny clumps and soon the only vegetation was lichen lying in autumnal rashes across the sheltered sides of boulders. The air was thin and spare. The smell of warm grass and animals, which had been a feature of our Rupal face camp, was gone and instead the air was sharp with the mineral smell of rock.

There was a simple shelter at the Mazeno La high camp. Four low walls surrounded a square of gravel where we could string up our tarpaulin to give us some protection. We pitched our tent beside it on a flatter part of the moraine. Inside the shelter there were piles of cracked goat bones, the remains of the pre-pass slaughters from previous expeditions. I wondered, when the porters said that the clouds looked bad, if they were nervous because we did not have a goat to kill to give us luck.

The mist froze in the air and fell as sleet. It lay in wet slabs of slush across the tarpaulin and we hit at it from the inside to stop it pulling down the shelter. As the afternoon rolled on the sleet turned to hail and the echoes of thunder cracked off the mountain. The storm was close to us. The cracks and flashes came simultaneously and it sounded like truckfulls of rock were being poured out of the sky. We sat in a circle under the tarp and gritted our teeth. When it sounded like it was directly above us I put my spare clothes between the metal pole that was supporting the tarp and the ground in an effort to make it less of a lightning conductor. I wasn't sure if it would help. Wind blew through the gaps in the wall and the rain dripped from rock to rock and puddled around the goat bones and the gravel. This was the kind of storm that could make an expedition into a disaster if its members were unlucky enough to be caught high on the mountain; for us on the pass, it was just unpleasant.

It was too cold to write my diary at the Mazeno La high camp. The next day and the day after I didn't write either, but for different reasons.

In the morning the tent was covered in a dusting of ice and my fingers were numb after rolling it up. I held them in my armpits and clenched my teeth as the blood returned to them, shooting pain across my chest and into my stomach.

The early morning steps were stiff and clumsy. My head felt tight with altitude and my stomach was revolted by the porridge I had forced myself to eat. In the pre-dawn dimness we couldn't see the pass.

'Maybe there are clouds?' Mirza was passing on the concerns of the porters. His face was pinched with the cold and he hunched his thin shoulders to keep the collar of his jacket high on his neck. 'If there are clouds we cannot go on because we will not see where the rock falls are coming from. Until they are hitting us…'

I knew I should defer to them but the weather had improved since the previous evening's storm. It seemed just as unwise to spend a day here because of cloud.

'Let's walk a bit further up and then have tea when we can see the pass better.' So we carried on kicking numb feet into the night-frozen snow. I felt a surge of excitement when the sun came up and burned away the haze that had gathered up on the pass. There were still clouds higher on the mountain but the ridge of the pass was clear and it shone in a clean white line against the deepening blue of the sky. We were in the shelter of the pass and, now the sun was up, the glacier turned from acting like a fridge to a reflective mirror. I stripped off my down jacket, rolled up my sleeves and put on sunglasses. Mirza had cheered up with the warmth and now he scanned the slope, reading it for the cleanest route up.

We climbed higher and stepped from the ridges of fallen rock on to the glacier which was run through with crevasses. Above us was the high point of the trek. We would be at 17,700ft on the pass. I clenched my eyes to clear the altitude dizziness and carried on stepping into the slope with scratchy crampon steps. I took two breaths to a step, then three, then a two-breath pause between steps. The dull drum of a headache began behind the bridge of my nose.

Over a false summit lip and the slope was shallower. We walked up a funnel-shaped dip towards the cleaner snow above. The angles were confusing because in the bright sunlight there was no difference in the shade of white to suggest the shape of the ground. My ice axe sunk deeper and I knew we were on the drifts that came from the spindrift that blew over the pass – not much further. Triple-breath steps, quadruple-breath steps, sweating, blinking pauses, then...

A new vista opened out below. We had been four days in front of the Rupal face, walking at the bottom of the longest mountain face in the world, but now we had turned the corner and could see a completely different face of the mountain, the Diamir face and the Chilas side of Nanga Parbat.

In the photographs of me at the top you can see my too-soon-joy. My Chitral hat is at a jaunty angle, my hands are tucked in the tops of my rucksack. I didn't know how technical the descent was going to be and I didn't know who would be waiting for us at the bottom. I thought I was through the worst.

The slope was shaded on the other side. Our crampons scraped on rocks that lay frozen into the ice. It was tiring picking our way down this mixed ground, more tiring than the ascent because each step was awkward and required concentration.

About halfway down our route was blocked by a line of cliff that ran all across the slope so that we could go no further without setting up the rope and abseiling down to the next patch of snow. Sher looped a sling around a nose of rock and threaded the rope through it. I went down first, using the old-fashioned abseil technique of twisting the length around my back and round one thigh as we did not have harnesses. My rucksack swung me round and I scrabbled my boots against the friable rock. I let myself down slowly with the rope tight and uncomfortable round my leg. The snow at the bottom was peppered with fallen rocks from the slope above. Some were large, and embedded deep in the glacier with a combination of the heat they drew from the sun and the force with which they had first hit. It was clear this wasn't a place to linger. The others followed and we pulled the rope through the sling while clustered beneath a semi-overhang to avoid any debris it might bring down.

Away from the cliff we relaxed a bit. We carried on past the glacial pools and gradually more and more rocks covered the glacier so that it wasn't quite clear at what point we moved from rock-covered glacier on to the rock of the mountain again.

Somewhere in the bleak piles of the moraine the men from Zangot were waiting for us. We didn't see them until we had passed them and they came trotting across the moraine, waving.

'We nearly missed you.' They called to us in Chilasi dialect. 'We couldn't see where you were. Normally the route is down the other side of the valley.'

Mirza's face tightened. Mirza was from Chilas and spoke their dialect but was cautious about the people who lived in Zangot, just as most people are cautious about the Chilasi people in general. 'The Zangoti men,' he had told me while we were planning, 'are the worst in the valley, but it is OK, we will avoid their village.'

'Peace be with you,' he said, then to me, quiet and serious, 'give these men many biscuits and cigarettes.' We all shook hands. Mohammed and Sher didn't speak; as Astoris they were cautious of these men from the other side of the mountain and looked upset.

'We saw you cross the pass this morning with our binoculars.' This was in Urdu; then they changed to Chilasi and turned their attention on Mirza. For some time it seemed they talked about other things. The conversation was measured and full of polite greetings. But in the long glances and in the solemnness of the pleasantries there was the message that something else was to be discussed.

Mirza had warned me that this might happen. Around Nanga Parbat the valleys are inhabited by many different groups and the people are territorial. If you walk through their lands they insist you employ them as porters. I had hoped to avoid this as we were not taking the normal route around the mountain and one of our porters, Sher, was the only member of our party who knew the way over the highest inner pass. I also knew that Sher and Mohammed were fit, well equipped and experienced. We didn't know anything about the mountain experience of these men from Zangot. Taking on new porters would also be more expensive as our current porters would have to be given half-wages for each day of the return trip.

One of the Chilasis was in charge; he had a long sparse beard so they called him Sufi. He got angry first. Spit gathered in the corners of his mouth and he argued with his chin pointed out, flapping his upturned hand. Mirza argued back: why should we take new porters, we had employed these porters for their experience. Sufi shouted back that this was Zangoti land and we must use Zangoti porters.

Mirza: 'We will not be going through your villages, we are going over the high pass.'

Sufi: 'It is our pass. It is our right to work it.'

Mirza: 'It is not your pass. No Chilasi uses this pass. You do not know the way.'

Sufi: 'It is within our land. Any pass beyond the Mazeno La is our right.'

The argument went on. Only the Astoris knew the Karo Pass that we intended to take; the Zangotis had no use for it, as if the starting point was Zangot it was quicker to go to the next village around the base of the spur. But when Mirza said this they claimed they knew the Karo Pass after all because sometimes their goats strayed up the path.

I was reluctant to give up the two porters that we had got to know and trust but the Zangotis eventually told Mirza that if we did not change porters they would beat our Astori porters in revenge. With ten Zangotis sitting around us it seemed we had no choice and reluctantly we agreed. I hoped Sher would stay on to show us over the high pass but following the threats he no longer wanted to be involved. The Zangotis chose the two youngest of the party to go with us. They were both sixteen years old and equipped with plastic trainers, shalwar kameez and a blanket each. That was all they had for crossing another snow-capped pass and all they had to sleep in at night. Our Astoris had jackets, climbing boots, thermal trousers and snow goggles.

I pulled Mirza aside. 'It is dangerous to go like this, Mirza. They will be in danger dressed like this. They will die of cold.'

'They are used to it.'

I turned to Sufi, who was now grinning having won the day's argument, and was counting the advance payment that had gone to him rather than the two boys who would do the job. 'Give them your jacket. And your socks as well.' Gradually the rest of them handed over clothes until the boys looked slightly warmer. Satisfied, the rest of the Zangotis left for their village further down the valley. Sher and Mohammed left too, striding back quickly the way we had come in an attempt to get back over the pass or at least away from the Zangotis before dark. The two boys were left standing beside the packs. Their names were Fida and Raji and they looked awkward and embarrassed now their elders had gone. We dropped down into the riverbed and walked for an hour or two towards the foot of the scree slope that led up to the next pass, the Karo La.

Evening came quickly. The sun dropped behind the ridges of Nanga Parbat and refrigerated air streamed down from the glacier. We had eaten a quick dinner of rice and lentils and were stamping our feet and drinking tea. I zipped my down jacket over my clammy shalwar kameez and pulled the rolls of my Chitral cap over my ears.

Fida and Raji were washing the pans in the still pools of the riverbed. Mirza had found out that they were distantly related and now they were eager to please and ashamed of the afternoon's argument. I had been angry that my companions had been replaced but that wasn't

Fida or Raji's fault. They were good boys, taking their employment seriously, pointing out each other's dish-washing faults. I clutched my enamel tea cup tightly to force the heat through my gloves. Everything was calm now. I remembered the pass and shrugged. It hadn't been such a bad day.

It was Fida who saw the stone in the air. I just heard a whirr and thought it was a gust of wind. It took me a second to connect the whirr with the impact of the stone on the riverbed, the thud and the tossed-up arc of sand. But by then Fida and Raji were already shouting and running towards the tent; calling to Mirza. They left the pans bobbing in the pool.

They were talking fast, Mirza looking up the moraine pile above the river. The boys were pointing and both speaking at the same time.

'What happened?' I asked. They carried on speaking in Chilasi dialect. The boys scrambled up the moraine slope away from the tent and Mirza followed them. For a moment it seemed I was being abandoned on the riverbank. I looked behind me at the stone half-embedded in the sand, sunk in like rocks we had seen on the glacier. I pulled it out of the sand and ran after them.

'What happened?'

At the top Mirza turned to me and said quietly, almost under his breath, his eyes turned away from me looking out across the valley. 'They say someone threw a stone at you. They say it was very close to hitting your head.'

'Who?' I still had the stone in my hand and I passed it to Mirza as if this might provide him with an answer. It was fist sized and rough with crystal deposits. 'Who threw it?' Mirza looked at the stone, and felt its weight in his hand. The boys looked at it briefly then turned back to scanning the valley in front of us. We could see up the path to the glacier and down a few hundred feet to where the path cut over a ridge and made its way to Zangot far below. We could see across the moraine field to the other side where it met another slope. There was no-one. We stood in silence for almost a minute, each of us scanning the boulder field. Mirza cupped his hands round his mouth and shouted in Chilasi, 'What sister-fucker is throwing stones?'

Fida picked up a rock and threw it across the field and it split and clattered. But there was no other sound. The cold made me shiver. I realised I had spilled tea on my gloves and my hands were now cold. Mirza thought he saw something moving and sent Fida and Raji to look behind a large boulder in the middle of the moraine. They went cautiously across, throwing rocks in front of them as if trying to flush out whoever might be hiding there. But there was no-one.

We carried on looking. Dusk was falling and Mirza mumbled, 'In this light the rocks make shapes.'

'There cannot be anyone here,' the boys said. The next village was almost two hours down the valley. It was nearly night. 'No-one from our village would walk for two hours in the night and there are no other villages before Zangot.' They talked some more in Chilasi.

Mirza nodded, and there was no smile on his face when he turned to me and said, 'It is from a fairy.' He looked at the rock that was still in his hand and threw it down. It split and let out a gravel spray of crystals. 'The boys say it happens up here. This is a place close to the mountain that belongs to the fairies.'

While the claim was ridiculous, at that point high on the glacial moraine with no villages for miles around the thought was unnerving. 'I think it is a rockfall, or that bastard Sufi,' I replied immediately. But there were no other rocks on the sand and Sufi was in his village.

We sat beside the tarpaulin, and without planning it none of us sat with our backs to the moraine slope. We sat until we couldn't even see shapes in the rocks anymore, just an inky blackness. I brushed my teeth at the tent door; I didn't want to go down to the river again. The pans were left still floating in the pool where they had been washed. When I got into my sleeping bag I wore my helmet and kept my ice axe beside me in the dark. I thought I might be kept awake by what had happened, but in the end the exertion of the day took over and I fell asleep quickly.

I was glad to wake up that morning. The fears of the night had left with the darkness but it was still bitterly cold and the sun had not yet reached our riverbank hollow. 'The boys must have been cold last night,' I called to Mirza.

He jerked his chin towards them and with exhaled smoke from the first cigarette of the day said, 'They did not sleep.' He paused then added, 'But they stayed...'

They were hunched beneath their borrowed clothes holding their hands around the pitiful flame of the gas stove. When they moved aside to let me pull the food boxes out they shuffled awkwardly, not wanting to stand up and expose their legs to the cold air. Their faces were pale and the cold seemed to pull the skin tight around their jaw. We ate our porridge quickly, standing. Then we packed up.

We were directly at the bottom of the Karo Pass. There were a dozen steps on the flat, across the mud of the riverbed, and then we were straight on to a slope which would only get steeper for the next three hours. I was panting immediately but I was glad to leave the campsite. In the night there had been no option of going anywhere, but now that we could leave I wanted to do so quickly.

'How many times have they been over the pass?'

'They have never been all the way over. Fida says that he has been part the way up once to find a missing goat.'

'Is there a path?'

Chilasi words were exchanged…

'There may be a path somewhere, but he did not see it because he was following the goat. We are not on the path.' Mirza smiled embarrassedly. He was meant to be the guide and he felt bad that he did not have experience of this route.

Unstable fallen rocks lay on larger rocks that in turn rested on the rock that was the mountain. This pass was too bare and new for earth. The slabs ground and shifted as we stepped on them but mostly they were still frozen together in the early morning frost. Fida and Raji ran ahead to get warm, their plastic shoes making a little tap with each step.

We climbed for an hour. The gradient increased and the rocks that we walked on got more precarious. Now I was using my hands with each step, my walking poles stuck into the waistband of my rucksack.

Mirza shouted at Fida for taking us on an impossible route. 'This is no pass. This has become a not-pass over the winter. There is no way through.' We sat and discussed what we should do until Fida found another fractured stair of boulders that we could inch up on again towards another blockage. With the Astori porters the only thing that concerned me was weather and my own fitness. But now, with the Zangotis, there was the new concern of getting lost and the prospect that we might have to turn back.

At one point Fida and Raji lost their nerve and sat on a ledge, and told Mirza that this was as far as the goat had come and maybe there was no way through. But by this time the prospect of going back was even more awful than continuing on up, so Mirza and I clambered grimly on and the boys followed.

It was a relief when at last we reached the dry rocks of the ridge. From here we could see the Daimir face, its rocky edge and central snow field, puffy with sculpted meringues of re-frozen spindrift laid down by layer upon layer of storm. Near the top the snow could not lie as thick, and pale blue creases showed where the cornice had bulged and avalanched.

The other side was a gentler gradient and going down we were tired and careless with our feet and let rocks fall, hopping and spinning with the smell of fireworks, then hitting the snow patches further down and sending up white splashes all the way to the bottom. The glacier gave way to firm ground. First there were rock slabs then there was dusty earth between the rocks and as the slope grew shallower the earth bore flowers and scrubby grass. It was still barren, but after two days above 13,000ft it was like a garden, full of colour and the smells of life and safety.

The Daimir face stretched above us and there, between teeth of snow-stuck rock, we could see the summit of Nanga Parbat for the first time – a small, unremarkable black pyramid holding a wisp of cloud and, because it was further away, looking lower than the white teeth around it. I wondered if the name Naked Mountain was accurate. The summit is naked in the sense that it is not covered by snow but it is protectively flanked by the surrounding tops and ridges, the peak only visible from one side, and then only just. Not like the self-assured pyramid of K2 or the rambling but obviously summited Rakaposhi. Rather than being naked, Nanga Parbat looked to me like a hidden mountain, a mountain in purdah.

We reached the trees and the air grew close and hot in the thicket of the forest – brittle dwarf willows with their skeletal curtains of branches, and the paper birches offering out curved strips of bark like toilet roll. Eleven hours after we had set out, we camped on the roof of an abandoned house at a forest settlement called Kachal. Exhausted we slumped against the mud-slapped wall to shelter from the wind. Weariness made the wind feel colder so I tugged my down jacket on again and sat in the sun. Mirza sucked at his cigarette and quietly told this story:

'This is a story about something that happened to me in the upper Rupal Valley, the camp we stayed in three days ago. Very early in the morning, while it was still dark, I was woken by someone shaking my shoulders. But I was in my tent alone. I went out of the tent to look but there was no-one around and it was cold so soon I got back into my sleeping bag. I lay awake and soon I heard someone calling to *salat al fajr* [morning prayers]. I was far from any village so I was confused where this was coming from. Again I went outside and I just stood and listened because this was the most beautiful sound I have ever heard, more beautiful than any music or singing or muezzin that I have ever heard. I followed the sound and found that it was at its loudest at a little nearby spring although there was no-one there. It must be coming from the water, I thought. I can still hear it in my head – the memory of this sound is the sweetest thing in my memory. It was a fairy call to prayer, and they can do this sound which is so pleasing it puts us in a dream and we don't know what we are doing. I realised that the fairy was telling me to pray, which I do not usually do in the morning. So although the water was so cold that it hurt to wash in it, I did wash in it and prepared myself. Then I prayed and after that I felt so peaceful and well. Many times since I have camped in the same place and I have tried to hear the call to prayer again but I have never heard it again. I will never forget it though, and I think I am so lucky to have heard it in my lifetime.'

This story was far more personal than the ones that had come before. In this and in the ones to come Mirza opened up more. Partly this release came from the new intensity of our trip. It had all been quite easy on the Rupal side but now our twelve-hour days and our porter problems had drawn us together with a sense of shared experience and discomfort.

I think there was another reason too. As of the previous night I had my own fairy story and was less likely to scoff when I had seen what the fairies could do. When Mirza asked me if I believed that fairies existed I didn't answer him clearly. Weeks later, back in town, I laughed at the thought of there being fairies and recited rational explanations as to what had happened. But on the mountain imagination and reality were blurred. It was like waking up in the night to a strange sound at the foot of the bed and trembling at the sight of clothes on the chair because they make the shape of a figure. In the haze of half-sleep and darkness, it is easy to think that the shadows and folds of clothes cannot be anything other than a hunched dwarf come in to frown at you while you sleep. But a second later, with the light on, the shapes that were so clear disappear and cannot be traced at all. It was the same on the mountain. At that point, slumped exhausted against the wall of the abandoned house, I thought it very likely that a fairy had thrown that rock at me, although a few days later back down in the hotel I could hardly believe that I had thought such a thing.

Another pass, the Kachal Pass, meant a steep uphill trudge from the first hour of the day. The slope was covered in a chaotic scattering of high-altitude flowers. Anemones with petals that ended in the curve-and-point of an Islamic arch. Yellow Himalayan Daisies, larger than the daisies at home and growing on thicker, hairier stalks. A local version of sage with leaves fine as babies' hair smelling of citrus and musk, which Mirza told me was used to make poison or, in smaller doses, to cure a child of worms.

We crossed another pass, this time in cloud, with a long but grassy descent. The grass gave way to pine forest and the path was covered in a slippery layer of needles. At the bottom a glacier-fed river tumbled from a snow cave. A final exhausting ten-minute climb took us to a tiny settlement that did not appear on my map but which I was told was called Kaloch Bak. Soaked with sweat and panting, I shook hands with each of the dozen children who had been watching my painful ascent. More gathered as we set up the tent. The girls watched from a boulder above us, safely out of the way. The boys sat near and watched us silently. The mullah made the call to prayer through cupped hands, facing down into the valley to let the men pasturing their goats know that it was time to pray.

Mirza's wife, who had returned to Korea temporarily after their wedding, had sent him a new digital camera. He now unpacked it and patiently took photographs of the children that lined up, holding the tiny screen out so each child could see the image. They hooted each time, and Mirza smiled lazily, his eyes closing half with laughter, half with tiredness after another long day.

'This is a story about my sister. This thing happened just before the festival of Eid. My little sister had been playing alone outside our house. My mother was very busy preparing the food and she did not notice for some time that my little sister had wandered away. She called me and my father and we went with my uncles and neighbour to look for her but we could not find her anywhere. It was getting dark and we were all very worried as she had been gone for many hours. She was only four years old and she had never gone away alone before. My mother was crying and calling out to her and none of us knew what to do. But then my mother heard my little sister call back out in the darkness and we all ran towards the sound. Every few minutes she called and we ran to the call. This went on for two hours and eventually we had gone all the way down to the main road, which is far from my village, and there we found my sister sitting on a rock. We could not understand how we had heard her call from all the way up in the village – it was impossible, but we were so glad to find her. I should explain that there were two fairies who were friends of our family. They were child fairies.'

I interrupted. 'Do you mean ghosts, children who had died?'

'No, these are not dead people. They are a different kind of creature, but they are similar to humans in their actions. My mother was always very nice to these two child fairies, she would leave them food and milk and they would sometimes sit and watch her cook and sometimes let her see them. They were my friends too, but they loved my mother because she acted as though she were their mother. These two fairies came and spoke with my mother a few days after my sister was found and they told her what had happened.

'My little sister was a beautiful child and the fairies had decided that she should come and live with them. So when everyone was busy with Eid they came and led her down to the road which leads to their fortress on Nanga Parbat. She does not remember them now, she just remembers feeling that she had to walk down to the road. But when the two child fairies saw my mother crying and so upset, they were upset too, because they loved my mother very much. It was them who called us down to the road and it was them who made my sister tired so that she sat on the rock. If my mother had not been so kind to these fairies then my little sister would have been taken away to live with the fairies.'

This story made me understand more about the Nanga Parbat fairies than any of the others or anything I read on the subject. Most of the stories focus on the mischievousness of the fairies. They appear to want to frighten or annoy. They use their invisibility to confuse and cause trouble. But this was only one side of them. They also have weaknesses for particularly beautiful or skilled humans and in this way represent the widespread fear that especially fine things are susceptible to misfortune. Most importantly, the fairies frequently have sympathetic relationships with humans; they interact with them and have similar emotions, and it is seen as worthwhile to nurture these relationships.

Now that our route took us through villages, we were expected to change porters at every village. I have a photo of each porter and when I lay them out next to each other on the floor of my study I can see their faces change and I can remember how the land changed too. Sher and Mohammed on the Astore side had Balti faces, with wide cheekbones and narrow Tibetan eyes. The Zangotis living at the foot of the moraine had hard, fierce faces, jaws clenched with the cold from waiting on the glacier for us. In Kaloch Bak they were still fierce, but less so. Across the next pass, to an equally small and unmarked summer settlement called Hua, the pasture was less rocky and the villages were set in the clearing of huge pine forest. Life here was more comfortable and the people's features were softer. They wore flowers in their hair or behind their ears and their skin was paler. The porters here were for short stages, so they sent young boys with us. One of them had light hazel eyes and looked identical to my little brother as I remember him aged eight.

For three days we walked along the northwest flank of the mountain: Kachal to Kaloch Bak, Kaloch Bak to Patro. From Patro we would climb our last pass, the Juliper Pass. We rested long at Juliper base camp. We ate the porters' cornbread and yoghurt and they ate our sardines and chocolate biscuits. I didn't feel like moving after lunch. The air was warm and the ground had hollows that were comfortable to sit in. But we dragged ourselves up the last pass, the last mica-flaked slope, the last drops of sweat falling in regular drips from the end of my nose. The top was muddy from the melting cornice so we sat on rocks.

Like a revelation another new face opened to us – the Beyal face – and with it a view towards the mountains of the west, more waves of the Karakorum. Rakaposhi, a huge gentle triangle drawing a bleeding line of clouds pierced with its summit fin. Then its opposite – the bastion of Haramosh, with near-vertical turrets, black because the snow did not stick to its steep sides. From the top of the Juliper Pass it seemed like the world was only mountains.

We paid off the porters, gave them the remaining lentils, rice and paraffin, and strapped what remained of our baggage to our packs for the final descent. We looked ridiculous with jerry cans hanging from our straps and rolls of tarpaulin and sleeping mats piled above our heads, but the porters could not come all the way down and still make it back over before dark, and it was only two more hours of walking.

The path down to Beyal had been destroyed by avalanches in the winter, so we struggled on cow tracks that meandered and doubled back on themselves or went down to attractive pools in the river to drink. But we were almost finished.

At Beyal there were huts for tourists. The owner lit us a huge fire and we ate spinach and over-ripe, cheesy butter which we melted in a bowl over the flames. All night rock falls tumbled down the gullies. They sounded so threatening that I expected the door to splinter open at any moment; as if the fairies were sending parting shots, warning us that we should not come back. In the darkness I could see the explosion of sparks from the tumbling rock. Beyond was the corpse-blue pallor of the Raikot face and above it a cinematic shooting star bursting into cinders.

The sun was out as we made the final half-hour stroll down to the real end of our circuit, Fairy Meadows. The heavy packs didn't matter anymore, and I let the blisters burst and burn because it didn't matter how bad they got now. The walk through pine trees reminded me of hot days in the Scottish Cairngorms, the white river running beside the path and the warm dust on the track. The smell was familiar, too – piney breaths came from the forest as the sun melted scabs of resin from the tree trunks. I remembered finishing the Lairig Ghru, a walk through the Scottish Cairngorms, and letting my sack tug painfully at my shoulders with the comfortable knowledge that after a mile I would dump it in the boot of the car. That was how I felt now on the final walk to Fairy Meadows. Mirza jogged ahead to and returned from the hotel with two cold bottles of Pepsi. He grinned through a beard that was wilder and woollier than the close-cropped version he kept to in town and we clinked bottles. 'We made it.' The celebratory photograph shows us both looking sunburned, weary and a little thinner than we did when we set off, but the relief of finishing the circuit shines through in our smiles.

There was a lawn at Fairy Meadows, smooth as a croquet pitch, manicured and fenced off from the horses and goats. We sat and watched the changing face of the mountain like a huge screen.

A sign on the lawn pointed to 'Killer Mountain'. From this distance it looked benign and peaceful, but it didn't always kill with fierce avalanches or storms. Often it was the impact of the altitude that killed climbers, forcing them into mistakes or causing them to linger longer than they should.

In an illustrated account of the Japanese ascent of Nanga Parbat that I found in the Fairy Meadows hotel, one picture shows what looks like two climbers fighting on the summit. 'He thinks that he is in a Japanese mountain lodge and Hiro has stolen his red bean cake.' In the photograph the climber has a mad, frustrated grin on his face and his ice axe is raised as if he is going to attack his fellow climber. He has reached the summit and he appears to be completely drunk.

Famed mountaineer Reinhold Messner related similar hallucinations that he and other climbers experienced on Nanga Parbat. One of the climbers on the 1970s German expedition was convinced he was walking down the mountain through fields of tobacco; Messner himself while descending with only one climbing partner was convinced there was a third climber in their group.

A single reality did not exist up there and it was hard to understand what the mountain could do to one's thoughts. Now that we were off the mountain, sleeping in beds, taking showers, drinking Pepsi, the fairies were unbelievable and I examined the thoughts I had had on the mountain with the bemused curiosity of someone who has lost his religion. And yet I remembered the fear I had felt going to sleep on the riverbank below the Mazeno La. After completing the first ever ascent, the climber Buhl wrote,

'The summit climb still seems unreal to me. It is like a dream, a dream that one cannot explain – so intangible and yet so real.'

Reinhold Messner *The Naked Mountain: Nanga Parbat – Brother, Death and Solitude*, English translation, Crowood Press, 2005

We drove down the cliff-carved road back to the Karakorum Highway. It got hotter and I sweated, but down at river level there was also the sense of physical relief that came from the thicker air. We stopped in Chilas for lunch and bought fresh fruit. There was one last stop before we returned to Gilgit.

All around Chilas the rock is particularly well suited to petroglyphs. Over time the rocks have developed a dark brown, slightly glossy patina. But when chipped they reveal a light yellow interior, so that it is relatively easy to carve striking designs on to them. I had come across a reference to a prehistoric river-god carving near Chilas and in order to find it Mirza suggested we visit a relative of his who had worked for a team of archaeologists who had visited several years before.

My legs protested at being made to walk again after the morning's rest and a couple of cramped hours in the Jeep. I hobbled along, stopping as our guide pointed out the yellow lines of the petroglyphs:

prehistoric, Buddhist, Scythian, and modern-day imitations done by the schoolchildren of Chilas. Each one showed its age by how dark the lines were. The modern children's carvings were still bright yellow, the Buddhist ones, over a thousand years old, had turned a tawny fawn and the prehistoric ones, carved perhaps another few thousand years before them, were dark brown.

The 'river god' was almost black and must be among the oldest of the carvings anywhere on the banks of the river. A triangular body ends in feet that look like a fish's tail. Its hands are splayed out and stretch down to almost touch its feet. The head sits neckless on the body, its features represented by a cross and with ten long strands of hair sticking up into the space above. It was just over a foot long. Looking closely I could see a carving of a human figure placed sideways halfway up the body as if it were swimming towards the river god. The figure was no bigger than one of the god's hands. What was the figure doing? Attacking a beast? Communicating with a deity? Or was it an unwilling sacrifice, cast into the river to appease a hostile god?

A short distance further on we came across another mysterious petroglyph figure with the same bristling hair. This one had no clear face and was wearing a loincloth with an animal tail attached and had what appeared to be a pair of symbolic breasts emerging from its armpits. It is described in archaeological texts as a Giant Demon-God, a suitably dramatic but vague name for an image we know so little about. It has lain for centuries spreadeagled on a rock near the much newer Karakorum Highway – a glimpse into prehistory that creates more questions than it answers.

We wandered back across the suspension bridge to Chilas. The water boiled around the concrete foundations of the bridge, the current making shapes in the water that disappeared and formed again, and I was reminded of the shapes we had seen at dusk in the tumbled rocks around our campsite that might have been fairies.

A Jeep roared past us, building up speed for the slope opposite with a wrenching crunch from its gearbox. It was just the sort of loud manmade noise that had pushed the fairies to their high-altitude sanctuaries.

CHAPTER 10

BALTISTAN

It was time to go upriver again. I always delayed leaving Gilgit, and following Nanga Parbat I felt like I deserved a rest, but after procrastinating for several days I caught the early morning bus to Skardu. We drove south down the Gilgit River then crossed it to the east bank on a colonial-era suspension bridge that creaked like old stairs. We skirted the most northerly curve of the Indus River in the half-moon bowl of its sterile flood plain and started up the Skardu Valley.

The valley running towards Skardu was the most constricted I had seen the river in yet. It burst and spat angrily like a confined animal and tossed spray high in the air as it crashed against enormous boulders in its path. The current here was so thick with silt that it seemed more like a torrent of emulsified mountain. In its depths it carried heavier loads and when we stopped I could hear that sub-aqua rumbling of river-rolled boulders. Streams cut into the river from the mountains above through vertical fault lines and added yet more volume.

I remembered how I had originally thought about making this trip by boat but had been put off by the logistics of importing or buying a boat and my own inexperience of such travel. Now that I had travelled most of the river it was clear what a ridiculous idea this had been. Going downriver in the Skardu Valley would have been like trying to hose a peanut through a sieve.

Sometimes I would see a village on the opposite side of the river and nearby would be a single wire with a pulley trolley hanging beneath it. These settlements consisted – as far as I could see – of four or five houses and a few green field patches in an expanse of gaunt mountain. On my map the area was blank – hundreds of miles of nothing and then a border with India. But what was really beyond the pulley and the fields, over the brow of the bare grey mountain? Where did the wandering goat tracks lead? Were there more houses, better pasture, or did the land stay corrugated and rocky?

In this steep valley the road was carved into the rock, a ledge half-tunnelled into a near-vertical cliff. The driver was going too fast, as minibus drivers always do. He probably hoped to make an extra half trip that day. One man, I think he was a Punjabi, shouted at him to take it easy but the driver laughed and so did the other passengers – they were used to it. I had morbid thoughts for four hours along that cliff-side wall, strangely, because it was only slightly worse than the Rawalpindi–Gilgit road which I had been up or down more than a dozen times. My mind wandered into fantasies and waking nightmares of what would happen if we tumbled and skidded here… or here. I imagined our fall, the seconds of falling, and the crash as we hit the riverbed. The drop was so high the bus would disintegrate on impact, and the hungry river would suck us up.

I was relieved when the valley flattened. We drove through apricot orchards, the trees lit up with the tiny orange fruit. In the cool beneath the trees were white flowers that in the shadows seemed to float in a layer like coagulated fog.

Women in brightly coloured headscarves and wide skirts moved between the trees, crouching to collect the fallen apricots and laying them out to dry in neat lines on any available horizontal surface; flat boulders, window sills and wickerwork drying racks.

The walls of the valley opened out further and we were in the broad, unexpectedly flat upper Skardu Valley. The river relaxes here, spread out in miles of conjoined lakes and abandoned meanders. It flowed through micro-cliffs of damp sand, like streams on a beach. At the edge of the road were grey dust dunes several feet high, shaped by the wind and feeding dust into the air. Nothing grew in this barren land; it was just grey all the way to the rough cliffs at the valley edge.

I remembered the river's mouth months earlier at the salt flats of Keti Bandar. It had been barren and grey because of the salt, neither land nor sea but something impermanent in between. Now I had a similar feeling up here among the grey silicate dunes. With the lunar dryness and the airborne dust it felt like this was half land and half sky.

I wanted to get as far up the Indus on the Pakistan side as I could but this was a sensitive area. From Skardu, the river runs a further fifty miles east in Pakistan before it crosses into India over the 'Line of Control', not an official border but where the frontline happened to be at the end of the first war between India and Pakistan in 1948. To the northeast is the Siachen glacier where the terrain is too hostile for either side to even agree on where they stopped fighting in 1947, and where cross-border shelling is still frequent.

The road to the Line of Control is still used to bring troops to the frontline. It is also used by the handful of UN troops who observe the ceasefire line. Mirza told me I wouldn't be allowed beyond the bridge at Gol, where the Shyok River and the Indus join, about twenty miles beyond Skardu.

I asked the hotel wallah in Skardu if I might be able to follow the road up to the Line of Control. He introduced me to Mansur, a young expedition porter. 'Wherever you want to go, this man can help you.' Mansur confirmed that the road beyond the police post at Gol would be difficult, but suggested that since the nature reserve of the Deosai plateau to the south was open to foreigners it would be perfectly reasonable to walk east and drop down to meet the road at Mehdiabad, which was on the river, fifteen miles upriver from Gol. But he said I had no hope of being able to see the border because of road blocks and the heavy military presence.

Mansur lived at Satpara. Although the village is a few miles south of Skardu and firmly in the middle of Baltistan, the people of Satpara are Chilasi rather than Balti. I noticed this when I first met Mansur – his features were visibly more Aryan than the more Tibetan-looking Baltis. The reason for this island of Chilasis in Baltistan is down to the actions of the seventeenth-century Balti king Ali Sher Khan Anchan. He was an extremely warlike ruler and in one particularly bloody raid he brought back prisoners from Chilas and settled them in a kind of prison camp by Satpara Lake. This group of prisoners never found their way back. Perhaps they felt safer under the protection of Ali Sher Khan Anchan. Perhaps the memories of what had happened to their people in Chilas made them never want to return. Perhaps they liked their crooked barley terraces and the fan of grey moraine with the view down to the deep blue waters of the lake. They stayed and remain an island of Chilasi-looking, Chilasi-speaking people in the middle of Baltistan.

I went to stay at Mansur's house in Satpara the night before we left for the Deosai plateau. The walls were neatly whitewashed and met the ground with a bulging slope as if they had been there for centuries and were feeling the slow pull of gravity like antique glass. A flower bed with pink poker plants was marked off with white stones. Inside, the ceilings were low and the floors carpeted with navy blue felt. A beautifully made window frame looked out across the valley to the pale-limbed poplars that marked field divisions on the family's small farm. His mother brought us tea and a cloth-wrapped parcel of chapatti.

It was a beautiful setting but the visit was tinged with sadness as a dam was in the process of being built and when complete the resulting reservoir would cover much of the farm.

'Where will the water come up to?' I asked.

'Over all this. The whole village will be covered. This house will be underwater.' He said this without any note of emotion.

'You will lose your house? Where will you go?'

'To Skardu. The government will give us money for our land. For every tree some money, for every field some money, for every house more money. That is why my father is building another house next door.' And now I listened I could hear from several places across the valley the sounds of hammers and saws, as the Satpara Chilasis built an extra house to double their money. I understood now why he was not sad about being evicted – this was a chance to start a new life in Skardu with a ready-made injection of capital. But it seemed a shame to me, that this little island of Chilasis, brought here forcibly four hundred years before, which had cultivated the barren moraines, planted poplars by their water channels and built little white bulging houses, were being moved on again.

It was a six-hour walk up the track to the Deosai Pass, which brought us on to the Deosai plateau proper. This is an extension of the Tibetan plateau, a 1,200-square-mile expanse all above 13,000ft. I had been higher when going round Nanga Parbat, but while the Nanga Parbat valleys plunged to habitable levels, the sustained height of the Deosai plateau meant no-one could live here all year round.

In researching this part of my trip I had come across ancient stories which told of the plateau's inhabitants being part-human giants who had left huge pieces of rock furniture and the foundations of giant castles. I asked Mansur about them. He laughed.

'No, not giants. You are thinking of the bears. The people who lived here, many years ago, were not giants but they were a troublesome people, like the Arab people today – you know, bomb blasts, fighting… The Balti king warned them not to cause harm to his people who lived in the Skardu valleys but they kept attacking and stealing the yaks and the children from the Baltis. They would eat the yaks and they would eat the children. At last the Balti king laid out a line of stones on the Deosai plateau and said, "Do not cross these stones or I will kill you." But the people of the plateau were very troublesome and they kept on attacking. When the Balti king saw this he sent out his soldiers and killed everyone on the plateau and all their animals. Their bodies were piled up and rocks were put on top of them. You can still see these piles of rocks on the plateau today. Since then there have been no people living up here.'

But there were still a few people who lived there during the summer months and on our second day we came across them. Their house was low and half dug into one of the low hummocks that rose from the plateau. In front was a dry stone enclosure several inches thick with goat droppings. The shepherds looked as though they had crawled out of the ground, with filthy clothes and ingrained dirt on their broad, flat-fingered hands. They brought us a bowl of sharp, cheesy yoghurt, and wished us a fortunate journey. But when I tried to talk more with them they just nodded or shook their heads in answer as though not quite sure of their own voices.

We only came across one other man on the plateau all day; he was from Katishoo, where we would stay that night, and was looking for a tso – half yak, half cow – that had strayed. He carried a thick bamboo stick and a small, cloth-wrapped pack of food and a blanket on his shoulder. We told him we had not seen any tso since the morning's river crossing – he would have a long search. How would he know it was his? 'It has a red cloth between its horns and a white circle on its forehead.' We wished him luck.

As we walked, Mansur told me about the expeditions he had been on. In his house he had shown me his father's portering card signed by the major expeditions that had come to climb the mountains to the north – K2, Gasherbrum, Masherbrum, Trango Towers. Twice it had been signed by the legendary Reinhold Messner. The reserved Tyrolean comment in the box next to it read: 'Portering to 4,800m. Competent.' Mansur himself had been on a Himalayan expedition with Wanda Rutkiewicz, the famous Polish climber, and told me proudly how after the expedition she had come and drunk tea in his house.

Portering here is a much bigger industry than around Nanga Parbat. The sheer number of big mountains means that there is far greater demand, and the walk in from the road to K2 is longer and requires more porters than the walk in to Nanga Parbat. This means that the Skardu porters are familiar with how the foreign trekking business works and what they need to do to ensure profitable work year in year out. Unlike the Nanga Parbat porters, they can porter as a full-time job and dedicate themselves to building up a reputation of reliability and good service. The market is very much at work and this makes it easier to organise an expedition.

Mansur was carrying a very heavy pack but he was stocky and obviously quite used to this. He strolled along with a kind of easy rolling gait wearing a too-big red puffa jacket given to him by climbers at the end of some previous expedition. It had seen a lot of use; the tired down stuffing drooped and the cuffs were greased with dirt to a shiny grey. There was a professional style to the way in which he hoisted the pack on to his shoulders, and balanced it on his hands in the small of his back. It was a style that I saw in many Pakistani tradesmen, the butcher, the baker, the kebab maker – they followed their father's trade and were absolutely familiar with the movements that they performed hundreds of times a day. The butcher jointing a buffalo leg, the baker rolling the roti on his fist in mid-air, the kebab maker executing an identical zigzag of sauce on each pile of chicken – it was all done with a comfortable, almost choreographed grace. Mansur had this too; he was only 26, but had been portering for more than ten years.

As we approached their rocky hideouts, marmots screeched and loped inelegantly to their burrows. When we sat to rest they reappeared regularly and shrieked again to warn each other that we were still around. These plump, slow-moving animals seemed unsuited to avoiding predators, but I suppose the biggest killer on the plateau was cold and to cope with that it helped to be rounded even if it slowed you down.

If we had kept on walking south we would eventually have crossed the desolate ceasefire line with India. Instead we turned north up the bare ground of the Katishoo Pass, which would take us back down to the riverside road. Rain came, large drops and persistent. We wrapped up and trudged on. The pasture and flowers couldn't cope with the exposure here and the ground was just mud and gravel. It was a dreary place. Grey snow tongues stretched beside the path, ragged and shadowed with mud. The underfoot grit was saturated and slippery. Ponds and pools and the oozing ground came together in a tiny stream. We entered the watershed of the Katishoo River, which empties into the Indus.

The horizon was punctuated with the glaciers of high peaks. Most of the water in the Indus comes from the melting glaciers of the Himalayas, the perpetual reservoirs of the subcontinental plains. If global warming continues at its current rate, scientists have calculated that by 2070 the glaciers will be reduced to such an extent that they will no longer feed the rivers throughout the year, and large swathes of Pakistan and India will become uninhabitable.

In a land of this scale, so unaltered by habitation or agriculture, it seems unlikely that humans could have any impact. These giant mountains and their glaciers look impervious to interference. And yet we now know that glaciers are retreating on many Himalayan mountains and that if this continues then one day the Indus will run dry.

As we descended from the plains, vegetation returned and the side of the valley, tinged with light green grass, had the sheen of chintz. We left the rain hanging on the pass and soon, in the distance I could see the variegated stripes of cultivation terraces. We had left the sky-lands and reached the altitude of habitation again.

Katishoo village felt like Tibet. The houses were square and painted white with regular, deep-set, ox-blood window frames and protruding roof beams. We drank tea from bowls, not cups and saucers as in the rest of Pakistan, and it arrived with a dish of tsampa – roast barley flour – and a spoonful of butter, which we mixed together in the bowl to make a thick malty porridge, Tibetan style.

We stayed with one of Mansur's friends, whose features looked both Tibetan and Chilasi, a mix of curly hair, high cheekbones, narrow eyes, stockiness and a hook nose.

We arrived in Katishoo on the seventh day of Muharram. In Skardu and the surrounding valleys the population is predominantly Shia, and for Shia Muslims, Muharram is the second holiest month after Ramadan. It is an occasion to mourn the death of Husayn ibn Ali, the grandson of Mohammed, in the seventh-century Battle of Karbala. The Shias consider Husayn to be the rightful successor to Mohammed and remember his martyrdom with huge outpourings of grief, demonstrated most visibly in mass parades of men beating and flagellating themselves on Ashura, the tenth day of Muharram. Every Shia mosque blasted out non-stop *marthiya* – elegaic songs – and in my hotel the television had been unplugged. Even in the taxis Bollywood music was replaced with the rhythmic singing of bygone processions.

We drank tea with our Katishoo host and talked about the approaching day of Ashura. There would be processions in Katishoo and Skardu and both men would join them. They seemed excited and tense, looking forward to it not as something enjoyable or festive but as something that was important and deeply felt. A tape recorder was found and we listened to *marthiya* while Mansur and his friend tapped their chests in time.

We left at dawn and were immediately caught in Katishoo's morning animal-traffic jam. The main street was deadlocked with goats. Because of the Deosai bears and snow leopards, every evening the shepherds bring the flocks back to the safety of the village. I had seen them the previous evening leaping blindly into low dark doorways dug beneath the houses. These semi-cellars stank of lanolin-warmth and ammonia but the houses were solidly built and in the upstairs rooms where the family lived the smell was not overpowering. Now with dawn, animals were streaming out of the cellars and heading back to the fields. We followed the scampering mass of animals until it fragmented to graze in the fields beyond the village.

The apricot orchards began again as we descended, the degree of ripeness of the fruit showing our height like an altimeter. First green, then as we went lower, yellow and hard, then orange, then reddish-orange so ripe the fruit dropped on the road from heavy limbed branches. We ate and ate as we walked.

Finally we reached Mehdiabad, the village by the side of the Indus, and here apricot processing was in full swing. The children gathered them in old shawls and brought them to the women who graded them into those that were good enough to eat fresh, those that should be dried and those blistered or bruised ones that would be juiced. They stoned them with their thumbs and laid the split-open fruit on drying baskets while an old man cracked open the stones on a rock and made great glistening piles of kernels. The kernels could be eaten raw, inserted back into a dried apricot to make a chewy sweet or crushed to make oil.

We sat and drank tea in Mehdiabad. The owner asked me if I had come to see the Buddhas. I had not heard or read about any Buddhas in Mehdiabad, but I said yes. Mansur didn't know where they were and now we had finished walking he looked absolutely exhausted; we had pushed ourselves quite hard to make the walk in three days. Some children passed on their way back from school and they were instructed to take me to the Buddhas.

They were not particularly impressive carvings; lines in the rock like those of prehistoric river gods near Chilas rather than the relief carvings at Gilgit and Skardu. More interesting were some stupa carvings which had been simplified and stylised to form geometric patterns. There was another Buddha, they said, further up the slope, so we climbed up on little hidden paths. We stopped at a shahtoot tree, a type of mulberry, where we spent a long time eating the berries. They were like blackberries but sweeter, stickier and full of deep red, blood-like juice. They were very messy to eat: they clung to the branch, you had to reach up to get them and the juice pods burst as they were grasped and sprayed all over you. The ground all around the tree was covered in the scab-like stickiness of fallen berries. Long dribbles of red juice ran from my fingers to my elbow and stained the cuffs of my shalwar kameez permanently. The boys told me that the berries are so messy to pick and that they rot so quickly that they cannot be sold in the bazaar. You can only eat them on site, beneath the tree, in old clothes that your mother will not be angry about.

They couldn't find the second Buddha so we went back, all of us red fingered and red mouthed like satisfied cannibals.

The river was not violent at Mehdiabad. It did not splash and boil here but there was still a sinewy power in the brown current. We couldn't see far upstream because the course twisted and hid behind apricot orchards. I walked to the end of the village, eager to go just a little bit further upstream, but where the houses stopped there was a police checkpoint and the road narrowed to single track. It seemed very little traffic carried on upstream and from here the route was closed to tourists. This was as far as I would go with the river in Pakistan.

PART III INDIA

KASHMIR AND LADAKH

CHAPTER 11

SRINAGAR

It was six days since I had left Skardu and I had spent five of them on buses. From Skardu I returned to Gilgit, retracing my steps going south down the Karakorum Highway to the capital city of Islamabad. From there I travelled southeast to Pakistan's second-most populous city, Lahore, and then spent a day crossing the border and travelling on to Amritsar on the Indian side. From Amritsar to Jammu the land was flat, crossed with wide dry riverbeds of rippled dust.

After Jammu came the Himalayan foothills, with a stubble of forest that grew taller and thicker as we wound uphill. As soon as the trees began, monkeys lined the roads. They sat on kerbside concrete blocks staring at the bus with pursed mouths and close-set eyes. There were the familiar Indian public safety warnings painted on the bollards: 'If you are married divorce speed – Do not gossip let him drive.' With the monkeys sitting on top of these yellow painted words, it seemed as though they might have written them and that those intent close-set eyes were admonishing the drivers as they raced past. When litter or food was thrown from a passing car any simian sense of authority was lost as they scampered after it and ate it two-handed or tore off bits for the babies which swung upside down from their mother's chests throughout the chase. The family in front of me had come prepared with sliced bread to feed the monkeys. The boy craned out of the bus windows to watch them fight while his sister carefully selected lone mothers or particularly small monkeys then aimed directly at them with well-meant 30-mile-an-hour slices of bread.

It was a shock when rain started falling in the mountains north of Jammu. It came suddenly in great heavy drops, creating snail trails on the bus's dirty windows. Then it came more heavily, making a constant drum roll on the bus roof. It made steam rise from the road, bringing up the smell of dusty attics and rusted metal. There was too much water to be contained in the stream beds and where there were no channels it ran flat across the hillside. When it reached the road it foamed in the blocked ditches and then abandoned the ditches to lie in droplet-cratered pools on the tarmac.

It rained all day and by the time it stopped we had reached Kashmir. Here soldiers had replaced the monkeys lining the road and the family in front of me had stopped throwing bread.

The soldiers' uniforms looked as if they dated from World War I, which gave me the impression that we were driving through a film. They wore shallow soup-bowl helmets and khaki puttees, armed with wooden-stock rifles that looked like Lee-Enfields or something similar. Sometimes they stopped our bus to search it but more often they just gazed at us with suspicious, cautious eyes as we passed.

We seemed to pass hundreds of army barracks as we drove to Srinagar. They were surrounded with barbed wire hung with pairs of touching bottles, a low-tech alarm device designed to jingle if someone tried to climb over. The window holes of the buildings inside were plugged with sand bags. At the gates were pillboxes and machine gun posts labelled with signs challenging the visitor PROVE YOUR IDENTITY.

Normally, towards one corner, set apart from the buildings but of the same sturdy construction, would be a temple marked with the Shiva lingam and the symbol *Om*, for soldiers love Shiva.

Shiva's destructive power is shown by his dance of death. It is said that when Shiva dances he is surrounded by flames. In the statues of Shiva these are shown in a circle, framing the leaping figure. Sometimes the statue looks graceful, almost feminine in its dancing pose, but this conceals the fierce apocalyptic power of the dance.

The mythological background comes from a story about Sati and Shiva. Sati was the daughter of Daksha, who was in turn the son of Brahma. Sati fell in love with Shiva but Daksha disapproved of her choice, as Shiva, although the equal of Brahma, had no possessions and spent most of his time meditating in graveyards. Sati disobeyed his wishes and married Shiva anyway. One day Daksha planned a great celebration and a huge burned offering to the gods. However, Shiva was not invited and instead Daksha set up a statue of Shiva which he cursed and made fun of. When Sati saw what her father was doing to the image of her beloved husband she was so angry that she burned herself to death by throwing herself into the flaming pyre. When Shiva heard that his wife was dead he flew into a rage and created demons from a lock of his hair that attacked Daksha and decapitated him. Shiva himself began to dance the dance of death and such was the power of his dance that the entire cosmos was in danger of destruction. It was only when the attendant priests threw Sati's ashes over Shiva that he was subdued into a long meditation which occupied him for an age.

Much later, Sati was reincarnated as Parvati, which means *she of the mountains*. She attempted to win back Shiva but he was still smeared in her ashes and deep in meditation, oblivious to anything around him. At last Parvati enlisted the help of Kamadeva, the god of love, and he shot Shiva with his bow made of sugarcane and honey bees. Shiva was enraged to be woken from his trance and immediately destroyed the god of love with a single glance from his third eye. With the god of love dead, the whole world became barren. Animals and plants were unable to reproduce and once again Shiva put the future of the living universe at risk. However, now out of his trance, Shiva was able to marry Parvati and she persuaded him to bring Kamadeva back to life. Thus the world was able to reproduce again.

Shiva's homeland has always been in the Kashmiri and Tibetan mountains. These are the lonely places where he is depicted meditating and dancing and these are often the places where devotees of his have come to live ascetic lives. These mountainous areas echo Shiva's fierce unforgiving nature and even more so now that they are full of soldiers.

The first view of the vale of Kashmir was grandly cinematic. We had been driving through a pine forest, concealed in the matrices of vertical trunks and horizontal branches. Then we reached the ridge and were looking down over the top of the pines into the vale: miles and miles of patchwork paddy fields, each flooded field a different shape and stitched to the next with a dry raised path. It looked as perfect as an architect's model – horizontal water-filled terraces describing the shape of the hill, contour by tapering contour.

The ground was fertile and overgrown. The roadside drains were clogged with hemp bushes which perfumed the air with resin. Everything spoke of a wet country: masses of tangled greenery, rivers tumbling over rocks, moss cushioning the riverbank and steep pitched corrugated iron roofs on chalet-like houses. Above the houses the fields were dark green, followed by the blue-green of pine needles and the hazed grey of cliffs.

I got into Srinagar in the evening. It was dark and from the shore of Dal Lake I could see the illuminated ranks of houseboats. Indian tourists arrive with bookings on luxurious colonial-style houseboats modelled on those built by the British, centuries before, to get around the property restrictions imposed by the Maharaja of Kashmir on foreign dwellings. In behind the floating tourist residences are houseboats where Kashmiri families still live and where less-well-off tourists can arrange cheap homestays. The homestay touts lined the shore road and thrust business cards and photographs of boats at me. A slight, wiry man tugged at my rucksack, '*homestay, homestay*'. He stared up at me from sunken eyes.

'Best homestay, cheapest homestay, my name is Toyyah and I provide the best homestay in Srinagar, the best in Kashmir and all India.' By now my rucksack was off and he was struggling under it, bending forward to take the weight but twisting his head back and jerking it in the direction of his *shikara*, a small open canoe. He paddled me out to his modest houseboat, showed me the kitchen where his wife was cooking on a gas stove, and his two children playing with plastic buckets at the stern. The toilet was reached by a gangplank and drained into a marshy reed bed. The guest room extended across the width of the boat and opened on to chairs at the bow.

'If you have just come from Pakistan, you must want to drink beer. Come, we will go and buy beer.' I was exhausted and ready to sleep, but

Toyyah was keen to get going and a beer did sound good. I had seen the shops on the road from Amritsar, darkened windows announcing 'BAR – AC ROOM – CHILLED BEER'. But that was in The Punjab; getting a beer in Srinagar wasn't as easy. Shops don't advertise the fact that they sell alcohol because this would make them more of a target to some of the violent militant factions of Kashmir. Toyyah, however, was confident that he would be able to track down an alcohol shop. We paddled back to the shore road, past the island where the central police station was situated, the water around it floodlit at night. I could see barbed wire defences sticking up between lily-pad islands. The fences were new, Toyyah told me, after militants had attacked the station with a boat full of explosives.

'Did you see it happen?' I asked.

'Yes, yes. I have seen many bomb blasts.' He pointed back to the shore. 'Behind those houses is the bazaar. There was a bomb blast there two weeks ago.'

Back on the shore the talk of bomb blasts seemed almost unbelievable. The promenade was busy with middle-class Punjabi families, eating from boxes of sweet rasmallai. There were strings of lights in the trees and hawkers selling plastic toys. We took a rickshaw to a closed shop next door to one of the bigger hotels. Toyyah rattled on the shutters but there was no reply.

'Don't worry, there is another place.' The next place wasn't a shop but a house at the end of a dark alley. The house was built on a hill and to get into the garden we had to climb down a ladder from the pavement. A veiled woman met Toyyah at the door. There were quiet words and Toyyah handed over the rupees I had given him. Something passed between their hands and Toyyah nodded at me to go back up the ladder. As we walked back along the alley he said, 'She had no beer. She has given us something to smoke instead.'

We stopped for food on the way back. I offered to buy Toyyah a masala dosa but he refused and as I ate he lay his head on his folded arms and appeared to shiver with each breath. I asked if he was all right.

'I am all right,' he mumbled, and rubbed at the bridge of his nose with bony fingers. 'I was working hard today and now I am tired.'

Back at the houseboat he came straight to the guest room and unwrapped what the woman had given him. I saw that it wasn't hashish as I had expected but a small grey-white lump of heroin. He took off his jacket and beneath his T-shirt I could see protruding collarbones and elbows that looked outsized against his thin arms. On the inside of his forearm was a scab, sticking out unnaturally with the white crust of infection. His long fingers were smoothing out silver foil and he produced a thin metal tube from the drawers behind my bed. As the smoke curled up from the crevice in the foil he moved the tube minutely to catch it all, slowly sucking. The sound was the hiss of a puncture.

'You go.' He pushed the lighter and the browning granules towards me. I looked at the bones of his outstretched arm, the scab and the eyes impatiently blinking. I felt sick and revolted. I wondered how I had got myself into this situation. I shook my head. He smoked again and almost imperceptibly, but definitely, he became healthier, or at least less ill looking. I remember thinking it was strange there was no smell. Now he was quiet and there was nothing to do apart from watch him collect the rising smoke from the silver foil.

He told me how he had started taking heroin with another tourist. The tourist had stayed with Toyyah for two months and called him Uncle. When the time came for him to go home he told Toyyah that back home he could not be able to smoke heroin anymore and that Toyyah should stop too because heroin killed you eventually.

But Toyyah had not been able to stop. Other tourists had come and they had wanted to try heroin too and they had given him money to buy it and help them smoke it, sometimes they even injected it. There was always enough for him too.

Some of the tourists who came later didn't want to stop when they got home so Toyyah had continued to post them drugs in return for money sent to him at the Western Union office. To avoid detection Toyyah hid the drugs in the papier-mâché ornaments that Kashmir is famous for and which he had learned to make as a boy. He took great care to ensure that the ornamental ducks and lamps were painted to a high quality so that they did not come under suspicion and he liked to think that his foreign customers were careful not to spoil the design when they cut the drugs out and perhaps glued them back together and displayed them to their friends. He sent the packages to the home addresses of his customers but with fictional names so that they could claim ignorance if customs discovered what had been concealed.

'You can do this too.' He gesticulated with the metal pipe that he still held in his hand. 'You should make this a second business in Scotland like it is my second business.' There was something unbearably sad about him describing it as a business. If he had been exploiting the foreigners and making a good profit from the service he was providing them it would have seemed fair. But all the money went on more drugs for the habit which he claimed was a byproduct of his involvement in the tourist industry. The situation felt like a quiet echo of what had happened in previous centuries of interference.

The houseboat that had seemed quaint and idyllic a few hours before now felt squalid. Toyyah left my room and I got into bed fully dressed and tried not to let the blanket touch my face. I remembered the weeping scab on his forearm and wondered how sick he was.

I thought now I could smell a sweet, rotten smell and I opened the doors to the bow and looked across to the shore.

Everything was quiet now. The lake was still and there was no sense that we were afloat at all. There was no sound; Toyyah's wife and children must have been asleep since we returned and it was easy to forget that they were in the next room. I supposed the tourists who came and took heroin with Toyyah must have forgotten about them too. A tourist's time is short and they don't always see the effect they have on the people and places they visit.

The next morning his wife smiled as she made me breakfast and she chatted with Toyyah while I sat on the plastic mat in the kitchen and ate bread and eggs. I wondered if she knew about his habit – how could she not know? I left a few hours later. I didn't feel like another night in Srinagar and had decided to go further into the mountains. When I paid him I told him it would be better if he didn't spend this money on heroin. He nodded and smiled and said of course he wouldn't, as if it were a ridiculous idea. I thought how pointless anything else I had to say was; he was already looking ill again.

CHAPTER 12

AMARNATH

I spent a few days following Indian tourists from The Punjab around the various sites of Hindu pilgrimage. At Mattan was a complex of temples set in a pine-fringed village that surrounded a natural spring. The Shiva temple was a pavilion in the centre of a pool, with a black lingam beneath a hanging brass water pot. Again Shiva was associated with the start of a river. The spring fed a pool of trout that the Hindus came to feed with popcorn. Signs read:

Do not touch the holy fish
Visitors, having done non-vegetarian breakfast/lunch
should not enter the temple and
the holy springs

The water ran through concrete channels into bathing pools where families were picnicking on multiple courses unstacked from stainless-steel tiffin boxes. All of this was watched by expressionless soldiers who sat in sandbagged bunkers, hands resting on heavy machine guns. Everything is a potential target for someone or other in Kashmir but a Hindu temple is a particularly obvious one.

Hindus say that the sun god was born at Mattan, and he is revered at several religious sites in the area. A ruined eighth-century shrine complex stands on a hill overlooking the valley, while closer to the town is the modern temple complex of Martand Mattan, organised around a natural spring, with the sun god's temple itself bright on the inside with walls of mirrors. In a shed nearby the god's many-armed, chariot-riding idol was being repainted in preparation for his annual festival.

Another bus, a shared minivan and an expensive Jeep later and I was deeper in the mountains at the village of Aru. It was getting dark and the mountains were murky in the shadows but I could just make out pine-covered flanks, rocks, the white slanting lines of rivers and higher up, beside the clouds, the luminous glow of snow.

I had travelled too far over the past week, down to the plains and deep into the mountains again, and I had picked up a cold somewhere. I rested in Aru, sitting on the creaky wooden balcony of a small hotel, reading and watching the post-school cricket matches while I nursed my sore throat and sneezed.

The news came up with the afternoon bus that there had been a bomb at Pahalgam. Pahalgam was where the Indian tourists stayed, a larger village, twenty minutes' drive from Aru. There was another Shiva temple here, sitting on top of another spring, and although it was small, it got plenty of visitors because it was at the beginning of a famous *yatra* (pilgrimage) path. Four people had died and a further thirty were injured. The bomb had been thrown into a popular restaurant on the main street of the town. There was a slight panic among the Indian tourists who had come up to visit Aru during the day: should they take rooms up here? Was it safe to return? But in the end they all returned to Pahalgam in the evening and the panic didn't last. Bombings happen so regularly here that they cease to be really remarkable.

To stamp their control, that evening an army patrol searched Aru. They looked threatening with their Kalashnikovs and an unfamiliar dotted camouflage. The Hindu soldiers wore black headbands that fanned out at the back down to their shoulders while the Sikhs wore jet-black turbans. They spread out in the hotel garden, walking backwards and scanning the darkness as they approached. Two of them walked along the veranda and knocked on all the doors demanding passports. They took little interest in me but quizzed the Israelis about their military service, probably more because it was something they had in common rather than because they were suspicious. I listened in from my doorway.

When the soldiers had gone, Faiz, the hotel owner, came up to see me and we sat outside on the balcony together and drank tea. I had not spoken to Faiz in the couple of days I had been in Aru. His younger brother tended to take orders for meals and Faiz seemed to spend a lot of time going down to Pahalgam on business. But now, in the dark, I felt like he talked to me as if we knew each other better than we did.

'I do not like to be in bed when there are soldiers in the village. I cannot sleep and I am sweating. Tonight my brother has gone to take the soldiers around the village so that they can make their search. The soldiers told him he must do this so that he will get shot if someone attacks. It is not good to do this. It can be dangerous but we have no choice when the soldiers ask you.'

I asked Faiz why the soldiers had come tonight.

'These are not the soldiers. These are very bastard men. They are the Rashtriya Rifles, who look for terrorists. Special Forces. They do killings, kidnappings. Not foreigners,' he laughed as if to reassure me. And then, almost to himself he said, 'They would not do anything if they thought you would see.' I realised at that point that despite being on my own with a scruffy shalwar kameez, few possessions and very little cash, my red passport meant I was probably safer than Faiz who had a family, a hotel and a business. It occurred to me that the safest place in the village might be beside me.

The patrols' uniforms had been different from the regular soldiers'; they were more modern but also more threatening and their guns looked newer.

'Why do they wear black headscarves?'

'It means they are ready for death. They came tonight to show they are not scared. They came to make us hate the people who put the bomb in Pahalgam. Life is hard because of this.'

'But life is good up here?' Aru looked idyllic. All the houses were of a good size and surrounded by generous fields. The forests were tall and the water was clear. It had a feeling of prosperity. But Faiz shook his head at this.

'Kashmir is not a place for having a good life. The army hate us because they think we are bombing them. Each of us is guilty to the army, even my five-year-old son. The militants hate us because we are not militants and they think we should be. It is dangerous in small villages like this because we can be easily attacked. It is dangerous in the larger places because that is where there are big bombs. There are few jobs and business is no good.'

Faiz's brother called over that he was back and the soldiers had gone. Faiz looked into the darkness but he could not see them leaving. Perhaps they had not taken the road and gone round the back of the forest. He didn't want to go back to bed until he was sure the soldiers had gone. His younger brother brought two *kangri* to us, clay pots full of glowing coals which can be held beneath the dressing-gown-like *pheran* that Kashmiris wear. We crouched around our personal fires and watched the road but there was no sign of the soldiers leaving so we waited some more. Faiz's brother sat with us. He was much more enthusiastic about Aru. 'The road to Pahalgam is better now. I meet my girlfriend on the bus to school every day. Our hotel has business again.'

But Faiz refused to be cheered up. 'We have tourists but this means we are a better target. The militants will never stop. Living in Kashmir is hard but we do not have a choice.' His younger brother smiled as if he were used to these depressive ramblings.

When the coals in our *kangri* were cold we went to bed.

The most important Shiva lingam in Kashmir, at the Amarnath Temple, is 8ft high and made of ice. It appears during winter every year in a cave two days' walk through the mountains. When it melts in summer the water from the ice lingam flows into the Jhelum, a tributary of the Indus. I planned to visit the cave but the pilgrimage season had not yet started and at this point in the year the valley was officially out of bounds to tourists.

Faiz, however, suggested a way around this. His other source of income was as a building contractor. He was due to make the journey with engineers from the public works department, to agree on the price for reconstructing the path to the cave in preparation for the thousands of Indian pilgrims who would use it in a few weeks. He said I could join him on this trip and thereby get round the restrictions.

There were eight of us in the party: two pony men, Faiz and four other fellow public works contractors (the officials from the public works department would follow later in the day), and myself. We had four ponies, two tents, and enough food to last us for a week.

We left in early morning drizzle. The valley began narrow and the path crept up damp black cliffs, zigzagging over gravel-covered boulders that the ponies took at an awkward lunge. As we walked, Faiz told me how in 1994 there had been a terrible snow storm and this section of path had been lined with freezing, dying pilgrims.

'I came along this path because my uncle was a pony man for the pilgrims and we were worried he would die out here. Everywhere here there were bodies. Some of the mullahs were saying it is good that the Hindus die, but to me we are all people. At last we found my uncle and brought him back here.' Faiz was silent as we continued up the slope, then he told me he had almost cried remembering what he had seen. 'I am glad this bit is over now.'

Remembering this experience, or the persistent drizzle, seemed to put Faiz in a bad mood for most of the rest of the day. Everything came out as a complaint; life was particularly cruel to him. The ponies were lazy, they had made this tiring journey so many times, and they plodded slower and slower like an unwinding toy. Faiz scolded his and kicked his heels at its belly. 'This horse is so slow. MY horse is the slowest.' He kicked again and almost overbalanced himself, swearing in Kashmiri. The ponies were used to the Hindu pilgrims from the big Indian cities and they didn't care much for their passengers. They were only scared of the pony men who poked them with sticks to speed them up. But once they were out of range of the sticks they slowed down again.

I walked on ahead. Away from the black cliffs the day brightened and sometimes the sun broke through the cloud. There were trees here and in among them it was quiet. I heard a clattering of pans as I passed a couple of nomad tents and I could look down on the sheltered place they had chosen, their buffalo tied to the trunk of a massive pine tree. At the edge of the forest I could see up the valley – gentle slopes covered in bright green grass, closely cropped to smoothness by the nomads' herds. Some camped but others had built seasonal houses partially dug into the turf; so that it looked like a flap had been opened in the side of the hill and propped up with wood.

As we climbed, the lushness faded and the ground was scabbed with rocks. Slicks of snow followed furrows down the hill and the path crossed them in a black streak of mud. At Sonmarg I saw the lake, a deep turquoise green with beaches of pale yellow sand, and behind it the serrated ridge of the Seven-Headed Snake Hill. This is the first camp for Hindu pilgrims and already the tent village that would accommodate them was being prepared.

We ate lunch at Sonmarg and Faiz told another story. In the height of the pilgrim season four years before, the camp had been woken by the sound of shooting. There was a militant hiding in a nearby concrete building shooting at anyone who appeared from their tent. Several Hindus were killed as they tried to run to safety. After a while, everyone stayed in their tents and for fourteen hours the militant shot at whatever moved in the camp. In a cruel ironic twist it was the pony men and porters who were camped in the tents at the periphery and it was these tents, full of Muslims, that the militant shot at.

'One boy from my village was shot in the leg, another was shot in the hand. This man here,' he pointed to one of our pony men, 'was in the tent but he was not shot. In the morning the army arrived and managed to shoot the militant. His grave you can see over there.' He pointed to a low pile of stones beyond the concrete building. 'We should not stay here long. It is a place I hate. This man will go to hell. The valley down there,' he pointed beyond the lake, 'is the valley of this militant. It is still a dangerous place because there are no roads to get there, so many militants use it as a place to hide. That is why I am scared of this place. Please take my photo here, in case I never come back here, I will be glad to never come back here.'

So I balanced my camera on a rock and took a photo of me mounted awkwardly on a white pony and Faiz frowning against the background of the opaque green Sonmarg Lake. With Faiz's stories and his perpetual anxieties, the camp which I had first seen as a staging post for a mobile festival now looked sinister, reminding me of newsreel footage of refugee camps.

The high pass made the blood pump in my temples and my throat rasped against the cold thin air but it no longer shocked me. I was used to climbing at altitude now; it hurt a bit but it didn't make me uneasy as it used to. I drove my feet into the grit or the snow and steadily went up. It was deep snow at the top, and when I waited for the ponies I saw that while I could walk on the frozen surface, their hooves sank in so that sometimes they wallowed on their bellies, blowing from flared nostrils, scared of the drifts that had swallowed their legs.

Faiz was now walking. 'The pony fell in. It is no good. It has hurt my back.'

In the high Panjtarni Valley, on the final approach to the cave, we passed a family of nomads. The father with a long beard grinned at me and nodded, eyebrows raised for as long as I looked at him as if we were sharing a joke. His three ponies were stacked high with pyramid-shaped, carpet-wrapped loads. On top of one of them, rocking with the load, was a young girl. In front, carrying more sacks, were the women, wives and daughters in conical red hats which sat on top of long plaits of hair. They wore aprons stitched with beads and coins and I couldn't tell which were wives and which were daughters because they were all carrying babies. Their goats were already at the settlement, two low-lying stone shacks with narrow doors and windows sheltering in the lee of some cliffs. Men sat around outside and stared at me suspiciously.

Another empty tent village lay across an alluvial plain. It was freezing and a harsh wet wind was blowing through the canvas tunnels of the tent. The men at the camp brought me a *kangri* and I huddled over it, pulling the ends of my *pheran* under my feet because the earth beneath the groundsheet felt like permafrost.

Soon it was dinner and Faiz's time to complain at the food, although he had chosen it. 'I cannot eat this peanut butter – it is a hot food.'

'A hot food?'

'Like almonds and pumpkin and all kinds of meat. It is bad for my liver and it will give me pain.' With a sigh, 'I will just have to eat bread. Oh, but I am hungry.'

The officials from the public works department arrived late in the evening when I was already lying in my sleeping bag, twisting in a vain attempt to find relief from the cold ground. When I woke up,

Faiz was breakfasting with them in the thin morning sun. They were speaking Kashmiri but I could tell that the negotiations had started; Faiz was gesturing to the lines of the path that passed the campsite, demonstrating their poor state of repair. Sceptical or resigned glances were already passing between the officials. I expect this was the point in the job when the real money was made and Faiz was rather good at it.

Faiz took me aside. 'My legs are too sore. I cannot come with you today. But I have paid a boy to go with you. It is bad for me, I will lose this money but it is important that you do not go alone.' I was quite happy about this, although I was pretty sure that the reason Faiz didn't want to come was because he had business to do with the officials – a day's worth of negotiation was more profitable, even if he had to pay someone else to do his guiding work.

'How much did you pay the boy?'

'Five hundred rupees.' Later on in the day I asked the boy how much Faiz was paying him and he told me three hundred rupees, which didn't surprise me.

He said goodbye with much embracing and handshaking and promises that we would see each other again soon.

We climbed up from Panjtarni on a narrow, cliff-cut path, then turned north into the bleak Amarnath Valley. Now we started to pass other pilgrims who had walked in from the road to the west, a shorter route to the cave but not the traditional *yatra* route. We passed three students in plimsolls. They carried their lunch of puris in plastic bags dangling from their fingers and each one had a bottle of Mirinda orange in his trouser pocket. Next we passed a group of soldiers in a mixture of uniform and casual clothes. They carried their rifles like spades over their shoulders. They told me they would be stationed here at the cave-side army post, which was there to prevent the kind of attacks that had happened four years before at Sonmarg. We quickly overtook a lone pilgrim dressed in a white gown and balaclava but with bare feet. When I saw him he was crossing a dirty glacier where gravel had been trampled into the ice. He walked slowly and awkwardly, trying to take most of the step with his heel. His eyes were hidden behind orange sunglasses and he whispered to himself as I passed.

In ten days' time there would be another tent village beneath the cave at Amarnath but now there were only a few tents surrounded by the bleached remains of last year's rubbish.

I could see the wide dark entrance of the cave above. The last steep climb was on concrete steps lined with railings. Two flights ran up the slope to cope with the huge crowds that circulated into and out of the cave. Later in the season there would be throngs of people, but now before the *yatra* season there were only a few other people here.

The smells in the cave were suddenly rich and complex after the spare mountain air. I smelled marigolds and rose petals, sweet incense, *bidi* smoke and the flavour of ginger and coriander from swinging tiffin cans. Iron arches stretched over the path hung with bells and the pilgrims set these chiming with the prayer to Shiva, '*Bham bham bhole*'. The *yatri* already in the cave shouted '*Bham bhole*' back down, loud and triumphant like challenges on a cricket pitch.

A line of shoes lay at the cave entrance; from here, on ice and gravel, all of us had to go barefoot. At the back of the cave was the white frozen lingam that I had come to see. It filled the apex of the cave, formed from a tiny trickle of water that emerged from an underground stream. It was bulbous and opaque white so that it almost glowed against the black rock. It had been strewn with pink petals which had frozen into the ice so that it was speckled with colour. Now I saw there were other, smaller ice lingams to the left nestling in their own crevices and I was told these were for other gods. The pilgrims pressed against the railings and handed bags of sweets to the attendants who passed them before the lingams and then handed them back. The railings were covered with photographs: solemn wedding pictures, passport photos, smiling children with the red tikka mark. They were tied with ribbons to the railing or pierced on to the barbed wire that protected the shrine. Many of the photos had already fallen to the ice to half freeze into the base of the lingam where they slowly fragmented then ran down the mountain with the meltwater.

I turned away and looked out of the mouth of the cave to the twisting rock faces opposite, bare like exposed muscle, snow lying along the line of the cliffs in narrow strips like the sinews.

A few steps down from the lingam was an altar full of statues and black- and red-smeared stone lingams. I remembered the other times I had seen these things – the tiny clay seal in Mohenjo Jaro, the small red lingam at the upstream end of the island Sadhubela. I remembered sitting beside the Sadhubela altar and feeling my head burn in the heat and the sweat trickle down my back. It was the same stubby phallus here, the same smells of incense and flowers, but I was over 10,000ft higher now and my bare feet were prickling with the cold of the ice. The repetition of these images gave me a sense of familiarity. It was the same feeling that I had from repeated views of the river, almost like a sense of belonging. I didn't feel so foreign when there were things I recognised.

Far beneath me I could see the white gown of the barefoot *yatri* as he took the steps painfully and slowly and I thought I recognised something in him too. The joy of a journey almost completed. The sadness of a journey almost completed. The yearning for meaning through a journey. Numb feet.

CHAPTER 13

LADAKH

The bus took two days to cross the Himalayas from Srinagar to the neighbouring state of Ladakh. Outside Srinagar the road picked its way between marshes and lily-clogged river courses. The Jhelum River gathers at the bottom of the Vale of Kashmir and lies in the Dal Lake and the Wular Lake before crossing the border and becoming a tributary of the Indus in Pakistan. The river was idle in the vale but as we climbed up and north it was angry again, encouraged by meltwater and steady rain. Snake tongues of snow licked down the valley sides to end in forks at the river.

When we paused for chai, everyone on the bus put on their *pheran* and sheltered beneath the eaves of the tea shack, breathing in sweet steam. Back on the bus the windows fogged up and the air smelled of damp wool. The Zoji La is the pass separating Ladakh and Kashmir and as we crossed this high point the rain stopped. It was like flicking a switch. An hour ago the land was green and wet, the windows were blurred with rain. Now it was as if we were driving through a huge dried-out quarry and the air smelled dusty again. We had crossed the dividing line from Kashmir, which experiences the monsoons of northern India, to Ladakh, which is part of the much drier Tibetan plateau.

Bare bones of cliffs emerged from steep gravel banks, and the world was all grey and infertile save for the pale green patches of barley clustered around settlements and carefully fed with irrigation channels. The houses quickly became Ladakhi-Tibetan style – flat roofed, with whitewashed stone walls and ox-blood red windows like those in Baltistan, because with less rain there was no need for the pitched corrugated iron roofs of Kashmir. The sun got higher and we passed a roadside Buddha carved directly on to a massive free-standing boulder. The swirl of the Buddha's braided hair looked like water. Covering the statue's feet was a simple lean-to temple.

We reached Kargil by evening. This was the closest I had been to Pakistan since I crossed the border several weeks before at Wagah, the only pedestrian crossing between the two countries, between Lahore and Amritsar in The Punjab. Kargil was not an attractive town. The shops and restaurants were run-down and most of the people I saw were policemen or soldiers. It felt like the unplanned suburbs of a bigger city but at the centre, instead of a heart, there was a truck stop. There was a hard coldness in the night and the sweet call of the muezzin competed with the barking of street dogs.

I ate dinner in the bus stop and fell into conversation with the bus driver. The road up to the Zoji La had been narrow and exposed and I congratulated the driver on his skill. He waved off my compliments and told me that driving this road was easy now, in comparison with a few years before. After crossing the Zoji La the Srinagar–Kargil road runs very close to the Line of Control. It therefore became the de facto border with Pakistan and a frequent target for the Pakistani artillery.

'In 1999 and before that we had to drive the bus very fast so that they could not hit us with shells.' A friend of his had died when a shell exploded in front of the bus he was driving. He had managed to stop the bus so that his passengers were safe but he had died a few hours later. The safest way was to drive at night without lights, then they could only hear you. 'Then you have to be a good driver and know the road so well. So now you see why I say that nowadays this road is easy.'

We talked more about the bombs and he pointed towards houses in the main bazaar of Kargil that had been destroyed by shelling. A whole family had died in one house. They had been relatives of his. The government gave money to build bomb shelters but often the money didn't make it to the families that needed it and if it did they didn't want to spend all their lives in an underground bunker. 'Many people left Kargil then. Who wants to live in a war, waiting for a bomb to drop on you? But what happened was that for some years it would be quiet and families would return and think it was safe. Then boom, there were deaths again.'

He told me about going to the Neelum River, which marks several miles of the border. On the banks of the river he would shout to his relatives who lived on the Pakistani side of the divided Kashmir. 'Twenty years ago we used to go there for a few days. We would camp by the river and then on some days the male relatives would swim across from Pakistan and stay with us in tents on the bank. Later they were not allowed to do that anymore and we just had to shout to talk to each other over the river. Always they brought presents. They threw the presents when they could not swim. Chocolate, cigarettes. They threw us K2 cigarettes.'

Many Kashmiris I spoke to talked about politics, how they hated one side or another or how they wanted independence. But the bus driver's experience reflected the complexity of the situation for those that live close to the Line of Control. Some Pakistanis threw shells at his bus and other Pakistanis threw him cigarettes. Relatives on one side lived behind the artillery and on the other they were killed by it. It was just an unfortunate situation. A horrible, unfortunate situation.

I reached to the bottom of my rucksack where I still had a flattened, half-empty pack of K2, which are particularly cheap and toxic Pakistani cigarettes. 'I bought them in Pakistan,' I told him. He took the crumpled pack from me carefully as if it were a religious icon. He examined each side of the pack and ran his finger along the health warning written in Urdu. He took out one of the unfiltered sticks and smelled it. It was slightly torn and some tobacco ran out on to the table. He swept it up with his fingers and poured it back into the pack.

'I have not seen this for twenty years. I think they have changed the picture of the mountain but they are still the same ones.'

'They are cheap cigarettes. They are not so good,' I told him with a smile. K2 cigarettes were not filtered and the tobacco was coarse and flecked with what looked like bits of plastic.

'They are no good you say?' He raised his eyebrows. 'I cannot remember. It is strange that they are from over there.' He pointed at the dim shape of the mountain slopes beyond the road that rose up to the ceasefire line. He sat still after he said this and said nothing and it seemed as if he were drinking in the night noises of motorbikes and dogs and far away in the bazaar the faint screech of Bollywood electro-violins. I imagined the sounds were particularly sweet to him as they represented a Kargil that was at peace. He turned the K2 pack once more around in his hands and passed it back to me.

'It's OK. Keep them. A gift.' I pushed them towards him.

'I can? It is your kindness.' And the pack disappeared into his pocket after a lightning-quick glance at the next table as if he didn't want to be seen receiving gifts from Pakistan.

In the morning we drove on and things became more resolutely Ladakhi and Buddhist. People's faces were high-cheekboned, eyes narrowed, and the average height fell. White stupas grew in lines beside the road and the cliffs were lit up with prayer flags.

The first monastery we came to was Lamayaru, set on a crumbling rock with the scattered white cubes of a village beneath it. Stacks of *chortens* – Buddhist shrines – stretched out in spiders' legs between the fields and stood like watchtowers on the monastery cliffs. The higher ones were decorated with white horses, peacocks and lions, and around them were the shrunken leather drums of prayer wheels, ready to spin as pilgrims made their circumambulations. Inside the building there was a smell of yak butter, and the sounds were dulled by the carpets and drapes covering floor and walls.

Legend has it that the valley beneath Lamayaru monastery was filled with a lake until Nimagon, a Tibetan Buddhist holy man, released the water to make fields. He prayed and made votive offerings to the Naga, serpent or water spirits, who burst through the gravel bank at one end so that the water could cut a channel down to the Indus which was only a mile further on. Without the water the dried lake bed made a sheltered and fertile valley where Lamayaru village now stands amid fields of pale green barley.

On the opposite bank, an hour further up the valley, was Likir Gompa. Likir means 'snake encircled' and refers to the twisting rocky mounds around the temple. In 1065 the fifth king of Ladakh, Lhachen Gyalpo, offered the snake-shaped hill to a Buddhist lama, and asked him to build a monastery there. Just as all the other water gods had adapted, evolved and been integrated into the next generation of religious beliefs, so this holy place of the snake king was syncretised and became a Buddhist holy place.

The monastery, with its rhythmic dots of ox-blood-red window sills, stood against a backdrop of snow-flecked hills. From the roof I looked down on the diamond-shaped mound which formed the snake's head – it even seemed to have a forked tongue, made of fallen rocks tumbling into twin streams. I looked beyond that to the hillside dappled with sun and snow and further down to the green-brown of the Indus. In Kashmir I had been away from the Indus for two weeks and now it felt good to be back with its familiar presence. It had been a long detour to get here and it was strange to think that theoretically, if I could survive the cold and the rapids and evade whatever security they had at the border, I could probably float down to Skardu, which I had left over a week before, and be there in a few hours.

Back at the Indus, the familiar motifs had appeared again. The belief in gods and snake spirits associated with water. I thought of Jhulelal in Sindh, the proto-Shiva who controlled the river at Mohenjo Jaro, the nameless monster on the black rocks of Chilas towering over the tiny swimming man, the snakes that shaded Swami Bankhandi at his ashram on Sadhubela, the mate of the Nanga Parbat snake that lived in the black lake and Shiva's cobra that he wore like a scarf. And now I added to this list the Naga at Lamayaru and the serpent spirits of Likir.

In Ladakh, for the first time in my journey, I had come to a place where tourism was expanding. Kashmir and Pakistan were largely off the beaten track but Ladakh was growing in popularity. I noticed it as we drove into Leh. Everywhere were hotels or the concrete skeletons of what would be hotels. I had come here as a student six years before and it had developed significantly in the intervening years. There had been one German bakery then. I had made myself sick by eating too much chocolate torte after a week's trekking (in a bid to save weight we had not taken a stove on our trek and survived for a week on biscuits and sardines). Now there were eight German bakeries and the shops on the main street were either carpet shops or internet cafés. Signs on the road advertised the experiences you could have in Ladakh. High Mountain Trekking – JEEEP Trekking – WhiteWater RiverRafting – Reiki Class – Massage Class – Post High Mountain Trekking Massage – Buddhism 2-day course. Ranks of Enfield Bullet motorcycles, those beautiful machines still made in Madras fifty years after the British company first opened a factory, and now popular for overland tourists, sat in ranks on hotel lawns. The Delhi to Leh road, 300 miles long and rising to 16,000ft, is the ultimate challenge for these vehicles.

I returned to the hotel I had stayed in six years earlier and hardly recognised it. The owner had put up a new building where there had been a tree-shaded garden and now he had Kashmiri staff to do the cooking; when I had first come we had sat in the kitchen while his wife baked puffed-up circles of Ladakhi bread on a gas flame. He didn't have any room this time, it was very busy.

One of the reasons why Leh was particularly busy this week was because one of the most important monastery festivals in Ladakh was taking place. Every year the monks at the Hemis Gompa celebrate the life of Padmasambhava, the renowned Indian-born sage. But every twelve years this festival is particularly important as the largest thangka – a silk picture using embroidery, patchwork and paint – in Ladakh is unfurled and revealed to pilgrims.

I had come to the Hemis Gompa by a wheezing, spluttering bus with standing room only, which for me meant standing slouched and bent-necked for two hours. Hemis Gompa stands halfway up a hill looking over the Indus. From the bottom I could see the lines of buses and trucks and Jeeps creeping up the hairpin bends to deliver pilgrims and tourists.

Every available flat space on the terraces, orchards and fields and the roofs of houses was occupied by tents: big parachute tents of restaurants, white square Tibetan tents of Ladakhi pilgrims and smooth-stretched, branded domes of tourists.

There was a bottleneck at the monastery door as the visitors came in both directions, crushing and stumbling to get into the over-filled courtyard. The upmarket Western tourists had arrived in fleets of Land Cruisers. Now they were crushed into this seething mass of bodies and some of them were employing their extendable trekking poles to force a way through. Inside they made their way to the 'Hemis Guest' enclosure reserved for those who had booked a place with the very best operator.

Most of the Western tourists were dressed in identikit trekking uniform: mushroom trekking trousers which unzipped above the knee to make shorts, wide-brimmed sun hats and matching photographer waistcoats with multiple loops and pockets. Each was slung with pounds of camera equipment. The ones with the laminated Hemis Guest cards set up their equipment in the gallery while the rest crammed in behind the barriers with the equally large crowds of Ladakhis. There they grumbled about health and safety, inadequate crowd control and the unreliable performance of their battery packs at altitude.

A fight broke out between some middle-aged Germans who had not been admitted to the special enclosure. The crowd turned to watch them shout and push one another. A broad-brimmed beige trekking hat was knocked off before some officials intervened and separated them.

The huge thangka had been unrolled at four in the morning. It stretched from the eaves of the roof down four storeys to the main door of the *gompa*. Thousands of silk scarves adorned the balustrade in front of it and when the wind blew down from the hills the thangka flapped lazily like the sails of a tall ship and the silk scarves fluttered away in ticker tape streams to land on the visitors like blessings.

At mid-morning in the packed courtyard the dancing began. I had bought a pamphlet to help me follow what each of the dances meant and in the crush I tried to read them and link them with what I was seeing – the Black Hat Dance or Zorchan; Mahakala (Gonpo Dance); the Dance of the King and the Ministers; the Dance of the Deer Buffalo; the Dance of the Nam-Tho-se – but I didn't know enough about them to follow the story or interpret their heavily stylised, symbolic actions. The explanations grew increasingly impenetrable – Nam-Tho-se has a darkish yellow colour and holds as attributes the Gyaltsen (the typical round banner symbolising the triumph of Buddhism) and a mongoose-spitting jewel (Nu-le). My hopes of identifying a mongoose-spitting jewel were slim so I decided to put my notes away and just watch. The dancers wore heavy embroidered robes and shiny lacquered masks and they swung symbolic weapons with each step. One of the deities was 10ft tall, its upper body built out on a wooden framework and supported on the shoulders of a hidden monk. This deity walked under a red-and-gold parasol and his golden face was symbolically fanned by an attendant. Young boys in gold cloaks walked behind the giant figure carrying an extended parasol and behind them walked monks with 6ft-long horns. The gods danced in turn, slowly, with stately hopping turns, bringing their arms in and out so that their wide embroidered sleeves covered and uncovered the skulls on their chests.

The monastery orchestra, composed of huge lollypop-shaped drums, oboes and long brass horns, increased the tempo as a new group of masked dancers skipped into the courtyard. They wore animal skins and skirts of rag strips over bare legs and they ran among the previous group of dancers, bumping into them and harrying them out of the courtyard as the bells on their ankles shook.

With each dance, the climax was the symbolic slaying of the devil, represented by the destruction of a red painted effigy made of tsampa dough. Sometimes this was done in a slow, measured way with careful slices from a sword and the dissected cake carried carefully away, and sometimes it was done in a manic fit of destruction – stamped on and thrown about the courtyard until all that was left was a brown stain on the courtyard floor. The animal-skin-clad dancers accompanied their aggressive destruction with handfuls of tsampa, which they tossed over the visitors in white explosions until everyone was covered in dust. The orchestra lost all rhythm at this point and just banged and rattled and blasted in a five-minute mad cacophony.

Sometimes I watched from the heaving crowd and sometimes I retreated to the rooftop where I was alone looking down at the dancers or out across to the river and the grey creased hills.

Skeletons danced, all white with eyeless, leering faces. They lifted the red tsampa effigy into the air and then cast it down on the courtyard. When it shattered they chased the pieces and threatened the crowds with it. They moved jerkily and when they ran off they let out a shrieking whistling noise and the big drums beat like thunder. They were followed by wild animals from the high mountains with backward-pointing curved horns. They killed the red devil by stamping on him with hooves and trotted beneath the flapping silk thangka to the dark of the monastery interior. Dance followed dance. The tempo rose and fell as the cast expanded. Each devil effigy met the same fate in different ways.

The afternoon turned yellow and it was time to roll up the thangka between sheets of ochre and red silk and take it in to be stored for another twelve years. Twelve monks laid it on their shoulders to carry it into the gloomy interior, piped in by oboists with puffed-out cheeks.

But there was one more dance, the dance of Hashang and Hatuk, the teacher and the pupils, which closes the festival. Eight boys in imp-like masks played the pupils and an old fat monk played the teacher, with a wide smiling Chinese face painted on his mask. He limped in, acting out his age, creaking into a chair that his pupils carried for him. They brought him his cymbals and he distributed sweets among them to prepare them for study. Then he played, alone because the orchestra had left with the thangka. The boys danced to the clink of his cymbals and their dance symbolised learning and study. They twirled their wrists and crouched down with arms crossed like baby Cossacks. They also misbehaved between sections, slapping each other on the head and tripping each other up. The pupils also killed the devil as all the others had done. They fought to tear at the barley dough and threw pieces at the crowds of visitors with a cricket-bowling action.

They kicked the remaining pieces at the crouching photographers and then ran into the crowds, clasping silk scarves round visitors' necks until they paid the ten rupees required to be released.

There was European Cup football on that night so the restaurants were full of tourists. All the talk was about the bus crash on the Hemis to Leh road. We had all come on that route in the afternoon. Everyone said the same thing: 'It might have been us…', 'I almost got on that bus but it was too full…'. It had toppled off the road into the river. The crushed remains of the bus had been pulled from the water, but there were few survivors. No-one knew who was on the bus but wild rumours circulated of tens of foreigners killed. That was the number that mattered. We all talked about it, seeking out details, fascinated by what might have happened to us. Beneath the rumour and exaggerated facts there was a swell of pride that we, the tourists in our photographer waistcoats, had faced danger and survived. This proved how daring our holiday plans really were.

In Leh I felt that hypocritical distaste for other tourists that I hadn't experienced in less-visited Pakistan and Kashmir. I found being among so many other tourists difficult. They got in the way and made me embarrassed by being tactless or domineering. I was one of them, and that couldn't be changed; we all went to the same places, ate the same food, tap-tapped away in the same internet cafés.

Another thing – I was lonelier in a touristy place. In Pakistan and in Kashmir, I was as interesting to the people I met as they were to me. We talked together because we were new to each other. But in Ladakh, I was just another one of the crowd and that brought with it a certain distance from those we called the locals. In Ladakh I wasn't strange at all.

I spent two evenings drinking rum and coke with a couple of English boys on their gap year. They were the same age as I was on my first trip to India six years before, when I had first come to Leh, and they reminded me of how I was then. They moved on when they got bored and averaged less than two days per destination. They planned itineraries on the flyleaf of their Lonely Planet and collected email addresses. They stayed in cheap, inconvenient hotels and they missed cheddar cheese. I envied them when they discussed next year's trip, also now being planned on scraps of paper (the planning was everything). For them this was the beginning of a year of travel, while for me September was the month before I started work again. Their discussions were on which countries, continents even, they might visit, while I had one small stretch of road left.

I wondered how it would be, going back to a desk and a boss. I wondered if I would cope this time; the last time I had managed two years. The boys wondered how they would cope with twelve months away from home, then there was university to worry about. I was lucky, they said. I had a degree and a job. When they got to that point, they said, they would be able to stop worrying. But of course we never do. We sat outside a German bakery with apple pie, yak-milk ice cream and Irish coffee, looking across the plain towards the turmeric-coloured Zanskar mountains, and we agreed that we really shouldn't worry too much because it has a tendency to spoil things.

I felt my way back along the unlit path to my hotel. When the trees blocked out the starlight I put my arms in front of me like a blind man and hoped there were no sleeping dogs on the path. In my dark room I pondered that advice – don't worry. It was right, I supposed, but I wanted to add, worry a bit. Because it is that slight niggle of dissatisfaction that makes us want to travel. That itch that keeps us planning itineraries on the flyleaf of our Lonely Planet.

With the festival over, I spent my final day in Leh down by the Indus, where the Kashmiri migrant shopkeepers and cooks came to wash their clothes and swim in the chilly current. The demands of the sprawling hotels mean there isn't enough water in the dry state of Ladakh to supply Leh's suburbs, where the migrant workers live. The water comes on for an hour or two a day, and in peak season not at all.

The rocks on the riverbed were slippery with strands of dark algae, water-swept like fine hair. I dipped into the water and let the current draw me down, bumping my knees against slimy rocks. On the bank I dried in the crisp dazzle of the high-altitude sun.

The next day I would go upriver for the last time. Two days up by Jeep, one day back, and I would be at the end of the Indian Indus.

CHAPTER 14

MAHE BRIDGE

From the road, the river below Leh looked light brown. Much less clouded than the opaque waters of south Pakistan, but still bearing silt. As we drove along its banks it turned to mineral green and beyond the army base at Upshi the water was clear. From here on up there were no big habitations on the banks, just tiny settlements, monasteries and the felt domes of nomad camps.

I had booked a Jeep and driver to take me as far up the Indian Indus as was possible. I had toyed with the idea of going back to Tibet, continuing to follow the Indus all the way up to the source, Senge Khabab, which I had got so close to two years before. But it was late in the year and the planes were coming less and less frequently to Leh as the snow crept down from the mountains. In less than a month all of the Tibetan plateau would be covered and virtually inaccessible.

The valley closed in after Leh and the road burrowed into the cliffs. The rocks showed off all their colours in the high clear sun. Red scree fanned out from cracks in the mountain so that it looked like the hills had been slashed and spilled their insides. Massive boulders fallen from above were black-red and shiny, as if still showing the effects of their volcanic birth. Where the river had carved its course, the smooth cliffs were the dull yellow of ground ginger while above the rock was sculpted into the impossible shapes of reptilian armour and burned meringues, creased with cracks and faults.

The road crept close to the river, no longer needing to go higher because up here the Indus was child-like and weak and it rarely flooded; I could have waded across it in ten paces. The Indus was young here. The slope of the course eased and relaxed into a small lake. The wind blew up the valley and carried the fine silt dust upriver to where it had come from.

We cut away from the river a couple of miles after Upshi. We would return down the riverside road, but to get there we would make a loop across the plateau to the south by the twin lakes of Tso Kar and Tso Moriri. A few miles on, plumes of steam came out of the ground as if from the funnels of a subterranean ship and with the steam came hot mud and mineral deposits. The road carved through lime-green chalky deposits that lay just beneath the surface like spilled powder paint, and further on was the white-crusted yellow of sulphur. With the minerals and the warmth of the steam the grass here was long and lush; its green seemed garish and unexpected on the high Tibetan plateau.

Tso Kar Lake was fringed with low white cliffs. I knew that the cliffs were salt rather than ice but I couldn't believe it until I stood on the crumbling edge and felt the dried-out granules between my fingers. The lake water was warm and fed into marshy land that smelled of sulphur and decomposing vegetation. The smell of salt and rot and warm water reminded me of the seaside. Far away I could see a black-necked stork, a wader that would not have looked out of place on the seashore, either. It is possible for this creature to live on the harsh Tibetan plateau because of the microclimate of the warm salt lakes and mudflats of Tso Kar.

We drove away from this unexpected warmth and it started to snow. The land returned to its monochrome bleakness.

We passed teams of road builders. Theirs was a purgatorial task. The first team collected rocks and laid them in piles 30ft apart along the road. The second team followed and broke up the rocks into chips that were then used to make the road bed. I had seen this done in Pakistan with a diesel-powered stone breaker, but here it was done by migrant Nepali labourers with hammers. They were wrapped in layers of clothing, hats and turbans of scarves but still they looked freezing, keeping their elbows close to their bodies and their heads down to keep out the draughts. For several more miles the piles of unbroken rocks continued. It looked like there were several more years of work still to go.

Now we drove through a valley of stone formations that looked like giant mushrooms standing beside a dry stream bed. It was evening and in the shadows of the valley their pits and holes looked like smiling faces beneath melted witches' hats. There were manmade devotional cairns too, circular and filled with rocks, each one crowned with white flat rocks inscribed with Sanskrit prayers. These cairns marked the beginning of a tiny Tibetan settlement. My driver was a Ladakhi and suspicious of Tibetans. 'Wild and dirty,' he said. But I persuaded him to camp by the settlement as there was a hot spring and a flat place to put our tent and I generally like being among people who live in lonely places.

Children with white teeth and dirty faces came to look at my tent. They retreated when the driver shooed them away but watched from a distance. They were silent except for sniffs from running noses.

A herd of goats trotted past, their horns painted in blue, red and yellow stripes. The largest, the leader of the pack, had tassels sewn into its ears and saddlebags lashed to its back. The baby goats were no bigger than cats and they bleated in distress when they got left behind.

There was a *gompa* above the village and inside the monks were chanting. They read monotone prayers from long rectangular parchments, chanting together, breathing in different places so there was never a stop in the sound. A tea boy went in every fifteen minutes and the monks shared their chapatti by tossing pieces to each other across the central aisle. Huge circular drums hung on cloth ropes from the ceiling. They gave off an occasional deep boom that momentarily numbed the sounds of praying. When the prayer finished, cymbals clashed and the long horns rumbled, deep and brassy like those of an ocean liner.

Silence, some tea, then they flipped their rectangular prayer sheets and began again.

We drove all morning, emerged from the valley at Mahe and there was the Indus again, smooth and narrower than I had ever seen it. There was a bridge, a teahouse and a police post. I looked up the river from the bridge: in fifty miles it would be Tibet, but foreigners could go no further. On a spur above the river a white patch caught my eye, a building. 'What is that?' I asked the driver.

'It is Mahe Gompa.'

'Can we go?'

'Not possible. Closed road.'

'It's not far.'

'Closed.'

'I will ask the police.'

I had had this same urge to go that little bit further up in Pakistan, too. But here I felt I had better reason; there was something to see up here where the Indus was young. There was only one policeman in the checkpoint and he was in good spirits. It cost me half a pack of cigarettes to go the final mile.

It was a new *gompa*, only 35 years old. Bright white painted buildings stood around a wide courtyard. In the kitchen we were given tea and shown the photographs on the wall: the Dalai Lama in discussions with George Bush senior, the Dalai Lama being introduced to the Archbishop of Canterbury by John Major.

'You would like to see the third Abbot?' a monk asked me. Like the Dalai Lama, the role of leader of Mahe Gompa is continuously occupied by the same being who is reincarnated over and over again to fill the position for several lifetimes.

'Of course.'

'He is tired. I will see if it is possible.'

We waited outside while the monk went up to the Abbot's rooms. He returned and beckoned us up to an atrium where there were thangkas on the wall, and a pile of blankets next to a bouncy ball and a tricycle with streamers on the handlebars.

'OK, you can come in now.' The driver went first; he had silk scarves to give to the Abbot and the monk took them and placed them carefully around the Abbot's neck. He received them wordlessly, a solemn look on his face. He sat on a raised carpet-covered dais. His face was wide and his thin hair was brushed over his forehead. He wore pink sheepskin boots with a cartoon figure printed on the heel. I looked at his solemn face and realised that the Abbot we were being presented to was a young child – three years old, I was later told.

Beside him was a half-eaten loaf of cake and a tartan Thermos flask. The monk passed him a handful of red threads and he separated them out and passed one to the kneeling driver and a second to me as I knelt before him. I looked up at him and he looked back with a constant, almost unnerving stare. Still he had not said a word. When I stared into his unblinking eyes it was the stare of someone much older and the idea that he had already filled this position for two lifetimes didn't seem so ridiculous.

As I was putting on my shoes in the atrium I looked up and saw that the tiny Abbot had come to his door to watch me leave. He tottered across the floor with his toddler's gait and stared with that unashamed, unblinking curiosity that children of that age have. This was the beginning of his third lifetime in the monastery, and more lifetimes would follow them in these small rooms high in his white, wind-whipped palace. The cycle stretched on and on like the geometric whirls of rivers on the thangka, re-circulating, unstoppable, even by death.

Outside, some of the young monks, aged eight or nine, were cleaning the steps of the prayer hall. They jostled as they worked and tripped each other up with their mop handles. A stooped old monk shouted at them, but when he had gone they giggled. When they got older, many of them would leave the monastery; when they reach their late teens, boy-monks are allowed to choose whether they want to spend their adult life there. The prayer hall steps were visible from the Abbot's window (there was one small window in his room that looked on to the internal courtyard). He would not clean the steps with those boys or laugh with them and he was bound to stay in the monastery. I wondered whether it was fair to have the same person in charge all the time, whether he would get jealous of the boys who were not as important as him. While it was undoubtedly a privileged position to hold, for a moment I felt sorry for that little solemn boy with all his lives stretched before him like piles of rocks.

We stopped by the river at Mahe Bridge, which was now bathed in the yellow light of dusk. Evening was a good time to be at the end of my river. My evening Indus hours were always my best. It was a time for sitting and thinking. A time for watching my only steady companion for this whole journey. The river set everything alive – it reflected the evening light, it drew animals and people and it made the ground around its course green. It was too cold for a submersion so I just dipped my head into the glinting water and watched it trickle out of my hair as it trickled out of Shiva's and back into the stream that had so far to travel.

I felt like saying a prayer but this river had received six thousand years of prayers and raised up dozens of gods and that somehow made any prayer I had seem inadequate. It was sad to be leaving. For many months I had led the pleasantly simple existence of moving upstream. In two weeks I would be sitting at the desk of my new job and computers, tax and commuting would take over my thoughts. My daily obsession with the river would be forgotten.

I looked down at the Indus. It was cold and clear here, it was a mountain stream, and I realised that for the first time in my trip I could touch my mouth to the water and drink. I bent – gulped and sucked, straight from the current like a yak. It was teeth-achingly cold. The taste was faint and was the flavour of rocks. That was all. I drank again and this time behind the rock taste were other tastes; rose water and incense and hard white sweets and gingery-fish and brown, sugary tea and throat-burning honey and the charcoal-crusted dough of fresh roti pulled from the tandoor. I swallowed and felt the coldness in my chest. I dipped my head to the river again and this time took a mouthful of Indus with me as I walked back up through the tall cottonseed bushes to the road.

EPILOGUE

Since I made this journey, in 2004, I have returned to the region several times. However, these subsequent trips have been shorter, often focused on visiting particular sites or people and have therefore felt quite different from the unencumbered freedom to explore that I experienced in those first long months in Pakistan. In many ways Pakistan remains a difficult country to travel in. While foreign businesspeople can now make their way fairly easily to the commercial centre of Karachi and stay in the sorts of hotels they are used to, large portions of the country remain on the Foreign Office travel blacklist.

Indeed, from the headlines I read in the international press it is painfully obvious why. The Sufi shrines which I travelled between in Sindh remain targets for sectarian attacks and in 2017 the shrine of Qalandar Shah, where I had watched in awe as the devotees danced through the night, suffered a horrific attack which killed 88 worshippers. The bombing was claimed by a branch of ISIL, which has, for the time being, replaced others as the most active and vicious terrorist group in the country. The Swat Valley also experienced several troubled years with the Pakistani Taliban temporarily taking complete control of the region and famously attempting to assassinate Malala Yousafzai in 2012. I often wondered what was happening to the mullasefs, the magic men of the valley with their unconventional, syncretic beliefs, during that time of fundamentalist Islamic rule.

Further north, at the Fairy Meadows base camp of Nanga Parbat, there was an attack on foreign climbers in 2013 which ended with ten dead. Reading about it I could barely believe that the peaceful, smooth meadows where I had relaxed after my exhausting circuit of Nanga Parbat had become the scene of such bloodshed.

As I travelled in the rare beauty of the mountains of Pakistan I often thought how lucky I was to get there before the hordes of tourists, but the tragedy has been that even a decade later tourism has still not taken off. Despite this, my friends at the Madina hotel in Gilgit continue to get by on the trickle of tourists making their way along the Karakorum Highway. The selfless kindness of Mr Yaqoob means he remains a well-known figure among those who have made the spectacular journey on this high-altitude road while Mirza, his business partner and my guide on the route around Nanga Parbat, now lives happily with his wife in Seoul, South Korea.

Technological developments have also changed travel in the region in several important ways. When I made this journey Google Maps had not been developed and along with a dearth of detailed paper maps this slowed my progress considerably. In some ways I envy the travellers who a decade later would not have the experience of turning up to cross a bridge that wasn't there, or are able to use a GPS-enabled mobile phone to navigate much more quickly and independently. But in some ways it was my limitations and the challenges of the journey done at that time that led me unintentionally to unexpected out-of-the-way places and into conversations with unusual people; and it was these serendipitous experiences that ended up being the most memorable of all.

The truth of this journey, as with every journey, is that it is unrepeatable; the land we travel through changes, the tools we use to travel change and we ourselves change. It is this I think more than anything that creates the powerful urge for the traveller to write their tales; to set down on paper what the place was like when we were there, and what we were like and how it changed us...

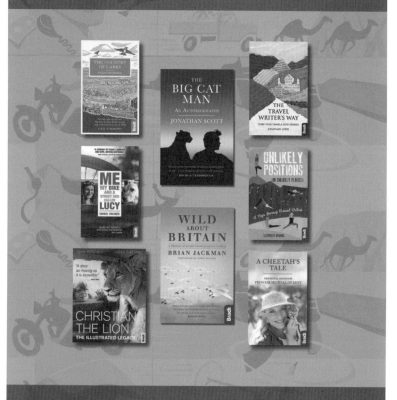